How to Write
Brilliantly

How to Write Brilliantly

A GUIDE FOR NURSING, HEALTH AND SOCIAL CARE STUDENTS

Deborah Miarkowska

1 Oliver's Yard
55 City Road
London EC1Y 1SP

2455 Teller Road
Thousand Oaks
California 91320

Unit No 323-333, Third Floor, F-Block
International Trade Tower
Nehru Place, New Delhi 110 019

8 Marina View Suite 43-053
Asia Square Tower 1
Singapore 018960

Library of Congress Control Number:
2024935256

British Library Cataloguing in Publication data

A catalogue record for this book is available from the British Library

Editor: Laura Walmsley
Editorial assistant: Sahar Jamfar
Production editor: Victoria Nicholas
Copyeditor: Ritika Sharma
Proofreader: Girish Sharma
Indexer: TNQ Tech Pvt. Ltd.
Marketing manager: Ruslana
    Khatagova
Cover design: Sheila Tong
Typeset by: TNQ Tech Pvt. Ltd.
Printed in the UK

ISBN 978-1-5296-7243-5
ISBN 978-1-5296-7242-8 (pbk)

This book is dedicated to my beautiful twin daughters, Sophia and Emilia.
May you be inspired in your academic and life journeys and make great choices in your
careers for the world around us. There is no ceiling!

Contents

About the Author

Deborah Miarkowska is a Senior Lecturer in Leadership, Service Development, Change Management and Clinical Supervision within Health and Social Care at the School of Education, Sport and Health Sciences at the University of Brighton and Associate Lecturer and Academic Assessor at the Open University.

Introduction

Are you a healthcare student in further or higher education and want to improve your academic writing skills? Then this guide is for you.

This is a supplementary easy-to- use guide that will support both undergraduate and postgraduate nursing and healthcare students to improve their academic writing and critical appraisal skills.

Aims

There are five distinctive aims of the book:

1 To simplify the academic writing process; bringing together the right ingredients to empower students to grow in confidence, to think and write critically in an engaging way with flow and cohesion.
2 To demystify the academic process in a clear and focused style.
3 To provide clarity to the requirements of academic writing for undergraduate and postgraduate Nursing and Health and Social Care Students.
4 To enable students to review their current approaches to academic writing and to apply several key strategies that aim to enhance their academic writing style.
5 To apply new models of reflective practice to enhance self-reflection and develop approaches to clinical practice.

Scope and Content

This book is for you, to provide you with additional tools in your academic writing, to enable you to enhance your critical thinking, to write according to your brief, to build your ideas with fluency and cohesion and to understand the process of developing an argument, with options, models, activities, top tips and check points.

How you approach, plan for, initiate, compile and deliver your assignments are key to your success. At both an undergraduate and postgraduate level being critical in your writing is essential and needs to demonstrate how you have engaged in academic debates and contemporary research happening in your field of study. The sources that you select and engage with, the way you show how they agree or disagree with other pieces of evidence and the manner in which you structure your argument will demonstrate your thought processes and how you have understood the information you have read is key to a high award.

The Personal Touch – The Ideas Behind This Book

Over many years, students have frequently highlighted how the academic writing process is not clearly explained and when studying in further or higher education there is an assumption that you should know the processes for attainment.

As a student your ability at academic writing is one of the main ways you are assessed to gauge your learning and higher level thinking skills; how we approach and deliver this can be a challenge.

This guide has one sole aim of simplifying the academic process; bringing together the right ingredients to empower you to grow in your confidence, to think and write critically in an engaging way, with flow and cohesion to improve your work and refine the processes involved in academic writing. I use reputable resources to explain this from reputable sources both old and new and designed by myself as each hold value in developing your academic understanding.

This guide clearly focuses on how you might rethink and refocus your current approach to academic writing with fresh ideas, models, processes and examples to critically reflect on how you might enhance their writing style and your approach to critical analysis and critical evaluation. This publication aims to simplify the academic process, to bring together the right ingredients to empower you to grow in confidence, to think and write critically, in an engaging way, with flow and cohesion.

I am a passionate lifelong learner and enjoy the challenge of writing.

My specialisms lie within Leadership, Service Development and Change Management in Health and Social Care and Supervisory Practice within the healthcare professions. I love my work for the potential it has to engage with others in a fresh and illuminating way, to impact how we work together and empower those around us. Similarly, I really enjoy working with students in support of their academic success and to enhance their professional practice.

I hope you find this resource engaging, easy to use and a great support to you in your academic writing.

The sky is the limit!

Deborah Miarkowska
MSc, PGCHSCE, PGDip, PGDip CIPR, BSc (Hons), RGN, TAQA, CPT
Fellow of the Institute of Leadership
Belbin Accredited Practitioner
deborahmiarkowska.info

1
Learning to Learn

Together in Chapter 1, we begin by examining all five aims in the book and explore the following themes:

> ## Key Points
>
> Together in Chapter 1, we will examine and explore the following themes:
>
> - The purpose of academic writing.
> - The knowledge areas required within the healthcare professions.
> - The skills to build, demonstrate and apply our knowledge.
> - The terminology requirements of your assignment criteria
> - Ways of developing effective reading and note-taking methods.

Let's refresh and unravel the purpose of academic writing:

The Why...

To be successful in further and higher education, you need to understand what academic writing is all about. It is a process to unravel, with a set of techniques to understand and adopt. This guide breaks this process down into a series of focused areas for you to consider.

Academic writing can involve writing essays, compiling reflective logs, report writing, portfolios, planning and reviewing case studies. In writing academically, you are expected to demonstrate your knowledge and to be objective, i.e. to explore the subject area in detail, impartially, with carefully considered analysis (levels 5–6) and evaluation (level 7) of the ideas of others and to provide your opinion and how this will impact your practice and settings; this is key to your success.

Crucial to the academic process is knowing how to express yourself, in well written, objective, academic English; with structure, flow and fluency. So let us begin with you and your current understanding and confidence in your academic writing.

Reflective question: On a scale of 1–10 how confident are you in your academic writing ability? One being the least and ten being the most confident in your understanding. In what areas do you need to develop?

Activity: Based on your scale, complete a Strengths, Weaknesses, Opportunities and Threats (SWOT) analysis of your current confidence and understanding of academic writing. What does it tell you?

Strengths	Weaknesses
What are the strengths in my confidence and understanding of academic writing?	What are my personal weaknesses in my confidence and understanding of academic writing?
Opportunities	**Threats**
What are the opportunities in my confidence and understanding of academic writing?	What are the threats to my confidence and understanding of academic writing?

Figure 1.1 SWOT Analysis – Assessing Your Current Confidence and Understanding in Academic Writing

We will explore different writing styles and unravel this a little later on.

Knowledge Areas Required Within the Healthcare Professions

At this point it is essential to both consider and understand how academic writing is all about demonstrating how you have built a depth of knowledge through the interpretation of theory and how we then apply this within our practice. We need to find our own method for doing this.

Firstly, in order to build and illustrate our ideas we need to fully understand the knowledge areas we are required to demonstrate in our health and social care practice and the skills we need to build our knowledge.

It is important to recognise that the practice of nursing and the professions aligned to health and social care practice is a holistic, human discipline and holds a knowledge base that we need to both comprehend and apply and remains steadfast across all eras.

Action: As you embark on each year of your academic studies take a really close look at your programme handbooks and module specifications. As lecturers we spend a significant amount of time preparing these and they provide really important pointers to students on what the programme is setting out to deliver and what we are looking for you to demonstrate. You will notice clear wording and phrases that will act as prompts for you to consider.

Ways of Knowing

The following discussion examines some key patterns or principles to consider to enhance your knowledge growth and application as a healthcare professional. The four fundamental patterns of knowing that form the conceptual and syntactical structure of nursing knowledge were developed by Barbara Carper (1978). These four patterns of knowing (that are still relevant today) include: personal, empirical, ethical and aesthetic knowing and whilst much debated, were viewed by Carper as important, as she argued that through the discovery of these knowledge areas (arrived at through reflection, synthesis of perception and connecting with what is known) professional practice could be developed and enhanced.

Check point: Why might the ways of knowing be important today? Arguably, the ways of knowing allow us to understand ourselves and our healthcare practice at a much deeper level; to appreciate nursing and the allied health professional practice as both an art and a science and to demonstrate to our patients why we are undertaking what we do in our practice. It provides us with a focus to understand more fully our rational for what we do in healthcare practice.

Let's look at how these ways of knowing and how they can assist you in your pursuit of knowledge as a nursing and allied healthcare student.

Personal Knowing

Personal Knowing refers to the knowledge we have of ourselves and what we have seen and experienced. This type of knowledge comes to us through the process of observation, reflection and self-actualisation. It is through knowledge of ourselves that we are able to establish authentic, therapeutic relationships as it propels us towards wholeness and integrity (Chinn & Kramer, 2015).

Reflective question: When you began to study nursing, what knowledge did you possess? Consider what you have learnt since – in your personal life, in school and through practice. This demonstrates your progression and growth in your professional identity.

Empirical Knowing

We gain empirical knowledge from research and objective facts. This knowledge is systematically organised into general laws and theories. One of the ways we employ this knowledge is through the use of evidenced-based practice (EBP). This way of knowing is often referred to as the 'science' of nursing (Chinn & Kramer, 2015).

Reflective question: Can you identify how your use of evidenced-based practice has enhanced and will further develop your professional practice?

Ethical Knowing

Ethical knowing helps one develop our own moral code; our sense of knowing what is right and wrong. For nurses, our personal ethics is based on our obligation to protect and respect human life. Our deliberate personal actions are guided by ethical knowing. The Nursing and Midwifery Code (2018) guides us as we develop and refine our professional practice.

Reflective question: Can you think of an occasion that you needed to make an ethical decision? If you are like many practicing nurses and healthcare professionals, you notice that your colleagues make ethical decisions every single day.
Action: Check the code of practice that relates to your professional body.

Ethical Knowing – Knowing Your Values

How would you define your values? What are the things that you believe in the way you live and work? Knowing your values enables you to make plans and decisions that honour them.

What does it mean to have values? Your values are your beliefs and principles that you believe are important in the way that you live and work and are central to who you are and what you do. They determine your priorities. Arguably, knowing your values are your guide to enable you to make plans and informs the decisions that honour them.

Aesthetic Knowing

The final way of knowing identified by Carper (1978) is aesthetic knowing. Aesthetic knowing makes nursing an 'art'. It takes all of the other ways of knowing and through it creates new understanding of a phenomenon. Aesthetic knowing is that 'aha' moment that we have when we uncovered something new; and just as an artist creates a painting, you are afforded the opportunity of new perspective. As an example aesthetic knowing in Nursing is achieved through empathy, dynamic adaptation and understanding of the components as a whole as well as the recognition of specific cases rather than holism.

Reflective question: Consider a time when you had an 'aha' moment. How did you come to that discovery?

Reflective question: Considering the four ways of knowing, how can each assist you in being a better person, a better student and a better nurse or healthcare professional?

Types of Knowledge

Now that we have considered the four ways of knowing, let us consider the different types of knowledge you may need for your programme.

Check point: Consider what are your current strengths and weaknesses in the following knowledge domains with your current studies? How will you demonstrate your knowledge to enhance your professional and clinical practice.

Factual knowledge is crucial to know in order to have an understanding of a discipline – in your subject area – where are your strengths and weaknesses?

Conceptual knowledge – Ask yourself have you considered the interrelationships amongst the basic elements within a wider picture that enable them to function together?

Procedural knowledge – Within your discipline what are you required to know? What are the criteria for performing skills, techniques or methods?

Metacognitive knowledge – How will you acquire the perception, awareness, understanding and discernment of your subject area and the processes we undertake to achieve this?

Professional Knowledge – Professionals define themselves in terms of what knowledge they possess and seek to acquire. Where do you need to develop?

Action: Check with your own professional body on the current knowledge and competency guidance that is relevant to your practice.

Understanding the Brief to Enhance Your Academic Writing

From examining the knowledge areas required of us in practice and that we need to demonstrate, it is important to consider how we understand the brief of assessments and assignments in order to enhance our academic writing.

Academic writing is unique to other forms of writing. Your reader (your lecturer or tutor) will assess the standard of your work against given criteria and you will receive a grade or mark and feedback.

The title of the assignment provides you with key clues on how to approach your work. Notice the language used and highlight the keywords indicated.

Failure to write by comparing, explaining, describing, critically, analysing or evaluating will result in a loss of points as you will not meet the assessment criteria.

Understanding Learning Outcomes

Learning outcomes identify what you as a student should learn and be able to indicate when studying a programme. They frequently relate to knowledge, skills, attitudes and abilities, and relate directly to how you are assessed. They are important for you to refer to as they often link to the marking criteria.

In the United Kingdom, undergraduate study is defined at Levels 5–6 and level 7 is for post graduate study.

One of the first things to do is to check the criteria that your organisation assesses you against and the learning outcomes by which you are being taught by. This is so important.

Proactively check your assignment brief and module learning outcomes. Understand them, break down the requirements, discuss it with your peers and tutor and keep a copy nearby with you as you compile your assignments. As you compile your writing, understand and refer back to the marking criteria regularly as a double check to the process you are undertaking.

Top Tip: Please ensure you know the criteria that you are being marked against, this will help you to design and formulate your work.

You may well be saying to yourself well this is obvious, and yes it is, but all too often students do not focus enough on the brief of their assignments and the module specification and do not fully address the needs of the assessment. As a result, this affects their overall grade.

We are now going to review and define the meaning of the keywords that frequently pertain to all assignments. Please take note of these and ensure you review the keywords of your assignments with the requirements of the following terms.

Activity: Pair up with a buddy and quiz each other on your understanding of the following key words.

To assess: Give careful consideration to all the factors or events that apply and identify which are the most important and relevant, with reasons.

To critically analyse: Give your view after you have considered all the evidence, particularly the importance of both the relevant and positive and negative aspects.

Comprehensively explain: Give a very detailed explanation that covers all the relevant points and give reasons for your views or actions.

Critically evaluate: Review the information to decide the degree to which something is true, important or valuable. Then assess the possible alternatives, taking into account their strengths and weaknesses if they were applied instead. Then give a precise and detailed account to explain your opinion. Use of the acronym SOY: Some said, Others said, you think is useful for presenting your ideas (more on this later).

To summarise: Identify/review the main relevant factors and/or arguments so that these are explained in a clear and concise manner.

Account for: Give explanations and reasons for...

Comment on/Consider: Provide your opinion. Support your views with the evidence you are reading.

Compare: Provide a discussion of the similarities and differences with a balanced (i.e. fair and objective) viewpoint.

Contrast: Outline the key differences between the subject material.

Define: Explain the concept in a concise way.

Demonstrate: Use key examples to illustrate an idea or concept.

Evaluate: Examine the value of something by reviewing the strengths and weaknesses before reaching a decision.

Explore: Thoroughly examine a topic from a variety of standpoints.

Identify: Recognise and List.

Illustrate: Show with examples.

Justify: Outline the reasons for and against the argument.

Prove: Illustrate how an idea is to be true through supportive evidence.

State: Express key points briefly and succinctly.

Describe a concept: Explain an idea.

Be concise: Be brief and to the point.

Deduction: This is the conclusion you come to after examining the facts.

Implications: The long-term view of something.

Role: The part something plays.

Significance: Give an outline of the meaning or importance of a concept or idea.

Validity: Provide the rigour, authority or soundness behind something.

Check point: Is your confidence growing in your understanding of what your assignment is asking you to do?

Ways of Developing Effective Reading Methods for Effective Study

In the following section, we will explore the skills required for effective reading and note taking.

Effective Reading Strategies

Rowntree (1976, pp. 40–64) still holds contemporary value in advising how we can get the most from reading in an efficient chunking fashion:

1 **Survey** – flip through the chapter or book and note the layout, first and last chapters or paragraphs, look at the headings used and familiarise yourself with the reading.

2 **Question** – ask questions about the way the reading is structured and think about the questions you will need to keep in mind whilst reading. Think about whether or not you think the book is relevant or if it's current and if it suits the purpose of your study.

3 **Read** – read actively but quickly, looking for the main points of the reading – don't take any notes – you might want to read through twice quickly.

4 **Recall** – write down the main points of the reading and any really important facts, and opinions that help support the main points. Also record the bibliographic details.

5 **Review** – repeat the first three steps over and make sure you haven't missed anything. At this point you might like to finalise your notes.

> **Top Tip:** Carefully select what to read and ask yourself if reading a particular source will be useful.

Within books use the contents page and index to find the precise information that is covered. Discover whether the author has used a range of references and sources. Within articles read the abstract, consider if the introduction provides a useful literature review. Skim over the conclusion to see if the paper is relevant to your question. Skim reading is about getting an overview of the information and looking for information that jumps out at you – examining keywords is crucial. Active reading requires you to think about what you are reading and the value and purpose it has. It is essentially about scaffolding of knowledge – i.e. linking what you already know with the new knowledge which can support a depth of under-standing and the development of new knowledge. Within your reading lists you need to be selective – ask your university library for guidance and support. Active reading should also be supported with active note-taking. Active learning helps us to make meaning from what you are reading and hearing. Careful thought and selection is the key to success.

Reading is like viewing a painting. You are looking for the structure and patterns in the whole picture.

Top Tips on reading and note-taking to build your ideas for independent learning
- **Building your ideas:** It is crucial to build our knowledge from a variety of sources. Read widely. Remember for every 1,000 words presented you might consider reviewing ten key sources.
- **Being fully responsive:** There are various methods of reading and note-taking and it is a combination of these that help us to get the best results with the least stress. Review, research and explore the methods discussed above and choose your approach.

Let's take a further look at note-taking methods.

Effective Note-Taking Methods

Effective note-taking enhances academic success – you are encouraged to experiment to find the best way for you. You are advised to consider the importance of note-taking. You could indeed argue that it is about increasing your knowledge of the subject, to explore and develop concepts in your mind, to understand and interpret information. Note-taking methods are important in making sense of the information and assimilating it.

There are a range of methods to explore, choose a method that works for you. There is no 'best method' but it is important to consider if the information is important, relevant and credible. Using a clear and structured approach may help you in the process of unravelling information in a useful way.

When note-taking in lectures it is important to actively listen, keep your notes brief so that you can maintain your attention on what is being discussed. It is important to write down key questions that may unfold from the lecturers so that you can explore these later. Leave space in your notes so that you can achieve this. Finally, it is vital to review your notes after the lecture, to reorganise and add information as needed.

Summary of note-taking styles:
- Linear
- Nuclear
- SQ3R
- Cornell
- Mind maps

Linear, Nuclear and Mind Map Note-Taking

Linear note-taking uses headings and abbreviations for main ideas and concepts.

Nuclear notes combine the structured aspect of linear note-taking with the visual representation of mind maps by connecting several lists to central ideas. Pattern note-taking starts from a central point and grows visually like a spider diagram, growing ideas, summarising points and showing connections.

Mind maps are a useful expression of ideas and concepts in a graphical form. As a simple visual tool, they enable a deeper level of thinking, support the structuring of information and support you to comprehend, analyse, synthesise and develop new ideas.

Check point: It is important to remember that effective reading and note-taking assists positive practice and this is in effect translated by the knowledge areas that we read, understand and assimilate.

As Keeling et al. (2013) point out that 'it is important that you keep records about the care you give in practice' and that 'documentation needs to be timely, accurate, concise and provides essential information'. Arguably critical thinking and the ability to decipher relevant and irrelevant information in the care of our patients is implicit within our practice and the academic process supports this. Active reading and note-taking is a skill that needs to develop. You will select and develop your own style and work out what works best for you and this process can be achieved over time.

SQ3R Note-Taking

SQ3R stands for survey, question, read, retrieve and review. It is a technique for note-making when reading, but could also work well for video lectures. It involves the following steps:

- **Survey:** skim the text (or watch the video) to get an outline/overview and develop a sense of which parts or sections might be useful. Note any headings and subheadings, along with things like figures, tables and summaries.
- **Question:** now that you have a sense of what content the text covers, what questions do you have to help lead you to do a deeper understanding? Your question could be 'what does that particular term mean?' or 'how might I use that information?'
- **Read:** now you have specific questions in mind, you will be able to read (or watch the video) actively in order to find the answers.
- **Retrieve:** begin processing and understanding the material by recalling the main points as if you were explaining them to someone else. You could do this verbally or in writing.
- **Review:** review the material by repeating the key points back to yourself in your own words.

The power of SQ3R lies in its ability to help students focus on the most important information with the texts by breaking the tasks down into manageable steps from survey-question-read-recite-review.

The first step is to **survey** the learning material to prepare the brains processing system. To survey the material, review the headings and subheadings in the chapter to activate your existing knowledge and skim through the materials.

The second step involves examining creating study **questions** by turning all the themes outlined from the survey stage into questions which enables you to study the uncertainties posed, head on.

The third step is to **read** and recall the text choosing information to answer the questions you have posed. You need to select the information carefully via active reading.

The fourth step involves you **recalling** and creating a summation of all the information gained by reciting it in your own words.

The fifth step involves a **review** of all the information recited which facilitates a depth of understanding.

Activity: Research SQ3R methodologies and reflect on what this means and how this approach might be useful to you.

The Cornell Method

The Cornell Method is a note-taking system devised by Professor Walter Park of Cornell University. This system consists of dividing a page into four sections including information on sources covered, keywords/questions, general notes and summary.

This method involves splitting the page into two columns, with the right column roughly twice the width of the left (this can also be done digitally). Detailed notes are written in the right column, and afterwards, key points, reflections, cues or questions can be noted in the left column. Space at the bottom of the page can be used to add a final summary. The Cornell Method of note taking is useful for developing your own thinking. This is because having a response column alongside a column for detail and quotes allows your thoughts and reflections to be clearly separated from the reading or lecture. It is also useful for processing your learning. Using paper to cover the right (note-taking) column, you can use the information in the left column as prompts to help you remember the detail or answers to the questions. Alternatively, you can cover both the right and left columns and use the summary as a prompt to jog your memory.

The Cornell Method also provides the perfect opportunity to follow the 5 R's of note taking, as introduced below.

- **Record**

Whilst the lecture is taking place, record in the main column as many important facts and ideas as you can. Write clearly.

- **Reduce**

As soon as possible after the lecture, summarise these facts and ideas concisely in the Cue Column. Summarising acts to clarify meanings and relationships, reinforces continuity, and strengthens memory.

- **Recite**

Cover the Note-Taking Area, using only your jottings in the Cue Column, repeat the facts and ideas of the lecture as fully as you can, not mechanically, but in your own words. Thereafter check what you have said.

- **Reflect**

Draw out opinions from your notes and use them as a starting point for your own reflections on the course and how it relates to your other courses. Reflection will help prevent ideas from being inert and soon forgotten.

• **Review**

Spend 10 minutes every week in quick review of your notes, and you will retain most of what you have learnt.

Activity: Research the Cornell method and reflect on what this means and how this approach might be useful to you.

Note-Taking Summary

Here we have examined various methods of note-taking. Have you found one that works for you for the list described?

Notes are important for the early steps in your focus and direction in your writing as they help you make sense of the text; they also help you make sense of your reading. It is important that your notes are structured, so adopting a system that works for you is crucial.

Reflective question: How will you streamline your approach and improve your current practice in building your knowledge, understanding the brief and the meaning of keywords and in using a note-taking methodology?

2

Getting Into the Mindset for Independent Study

Key Points

Together in Chapter 2, we will examine and explore the following themes:

- Think about things differently by redefining your mindset.
- Becoming an active and effective learner.
- Know thyself and your learning style.
- Developing a critical mindset and critical thinking skills to appraise and develop our ideas.
- Selecting and applying critical reflective models to enhance your practice.

Within Chapter 2, we will review our approach to independent study and consider the attitude required for effective academic success. Key evidence suggests (Dweck, 2012, 2015) that your mindset is key to your success in developing your academic writing and approach to learning. We examine key top tips in this area as evidence suggests that abilities are not fixed, it's your attitude that plays a key part in your success.

In Chapter 2, we will also examine the value of reflection as a tool for developing critical thinking skills and how a critical mindset enables you to build your knowledge to translate theory to practice and in developing fresh and innovative ways of enhancing clinical practice.

Together, we will look at independent study skills and how we develop as active learners via motivational and reflective tools including the work of Professor Carole Dweck of Stanford University (Figure 2.1).

Figure 2.1   Fixed and Growth Mindset

Think About Things Differently by Defining Your Mindset

Introducing the work of Professor Carole Dweck of Stanford University.

Carol Dweck, Professor of Psychology, Stanford University, has demonstrated some extraordinary insights in the field of developmental learning and the influence of attitude, resilience and motivation in transforming the meaning of effort and difficulty in the learning process.

In a nutshell Professor Dweck indicates that the ingredients for success combine effort, our ability to keep going and being motivated.

Whilst academic writing can be challenging, it is important to acknowledge that our approach determines the outcome.

Dweck emphasises from her work, that our abilities are not fixed, that they can grow and be developed (Dweck, 2012, 2015). Dweck emphasises that our powerful beliefs affect what we want within our lives and whether you achieve this. How we think is key and recognising and developing our mindset is your key to your success and how we act and grow. So don't lose heart. With a growth mindset, effort, focus, determination, we can achieve great things and we don't need to be held back by our fixed mindsets.

As Dweck indicates, 'A growth mindset is the belief that you can cultivate and improve upon your abilities through practice and effort'.

Activity: Reflect on a recent academic challenge and where you didn't do so well.

What did you do when you experienced this situation? Did you have a negative (fixed) or positive (growth) response?

Dweck (2010, 2012, 2015) argues that we can change the perception of our success.

So How Do We Become an Active and Effective Learner?

Active Learning is crucial as it enables us to understand texts, to understand the wider picture and to come up with our own thoughts and ideas that we can apply to practice. If we are going to develop skills in synthesising and analysing information from the texts we read, it is important to become an active learner and to begin a process of discovering, processing and applying information.

Check point: You need to consider how active and proactive you are in your approach to learning. Our attitude and approach are vital in learning, especially when it gets tough and in considering how we will demonstrate our ideas.

It is fascinating that the latest research indicates that our ability to think, act and pursue your own studies autonomously with resilience and motivation are key to academic success. This approach has the dual benefit of developing transferable workplace skills; including the ability to stay motivated, using initiative, organisational, time management and multi-tasking abilities and effective reading and writing skills (Dweck, 2012, 2015).

Top Tips on How to Put Independent Study Skills and Active Learning Into Action

Following the simple tips below will help to develop your skills and confidence in your study.

Active Reading

When reading, place close attention to keywords and phrases and to their meaning. How will this develop your arguments?

Gaining Independence

Gain confidence by working independently, set goals and develop your organisational planning skills.

Using Wide Sources

When researching, draw on a breadth of resources.

Being Persistent

If you are feeling challenged, persist in your efforts and refine your learning methods. Think growth mindset.

Seeking Support

Independent learning is seen as integral to higher education, but if you need help – just ask your personal tutor or academic supervisors.

Goal Setting

Set your goals, stay focused on your milestones and aspirations (Figure 2.2).

Action: Research Carol Dweck's work further to gain further insights.

You may wish to explore further the 5E learning cycle, a model first developed by Robert Karpus in the late 1960s. It is effective because it uses active training

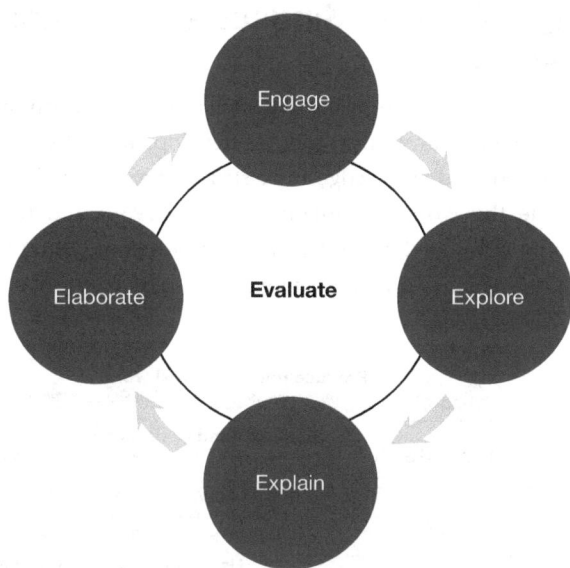

Figure 2.2 5e Learning Cycle

techniques, known as learning by doing. As a learner you apply the learning materials and your experience into your contexts.

Know Thyself and Your Learning Style

A learning style indicates your preferred approach to learning. Arguably knowing your own learning style supports you in achieving to the very best of your ability and enables your process of learning and enhances your engagement.

The VARK Model identifies four primary learning style, visual, auditory, reading and writing and kinaesthetic (learning by doing).

What Learning Style do you prefer?

Action: Try the VARK Questionnaire (www.vark-learn.com/the-vark-questionnaire) to discover more about yourself and how you learn best.

Developing a Critical Mindset and Critical Thinking Skills

So far we have looked at the knowledge areas required in health and social care practice. Our next focus lies within how we develop the skills for building and demonstrating the required knowledge and a structure to achieve this. With this in mind, we examine the work of Benjamin Bloom (1956) and the revisions of Bloom's Taxonomy developed by Anderson and Krathwohl (2001) to scaffold the depth of our knowledge and understanding (Figure 2.3).

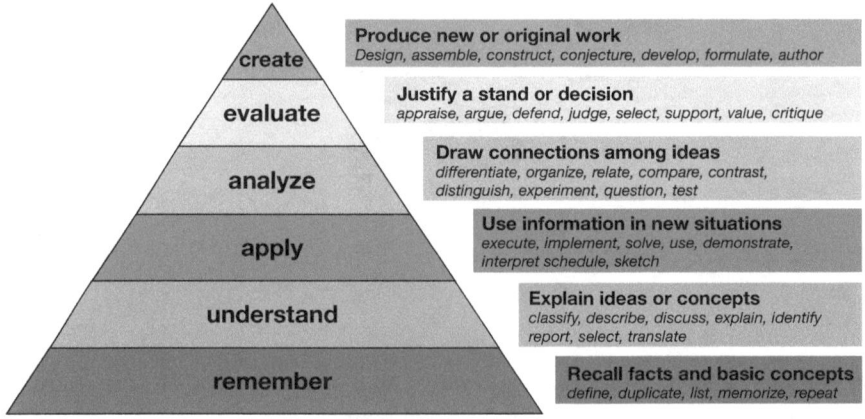

Figure 2.3 Bloom's Taxonomy

Earlier work of Benjamin Bloom (1956) identified a set of skills seen as essential for university study, the creation and development of knowledge and critical appraisal skills. Anderson and Krathwohl (2001) revised the original taxonomy by moving the evaluation stage down a level and enhancing the value of creativity as the highest domain.

What this pyramid is aiming to do is to illustrate how you can consider building and demonstrating the depth of your understanding, to become more critically aware in your academic approach and to create new and innovative ways to deliver your clinical practice. Let's unravel Bloom's Taxonomy and how you can assess your current thinking and approach to your academic studies to develop your critical appraisal skills.

As you will notice the bottom of the pyramid are the key skills of **remembering and understanding**. It is particularly important in scientific disciplines to be able to describe processes with clarity and precision and to convey complex ideas accurately, concisely and clearly. Questions will require you to understand, define, identify, label, name, predict, interpret, summarise, translate and provide examples. In addition, you will need to develop further critical thinking skills in the following:

- **Application** involves you illustrating how to apply x to situation y for example. How can it be used?
- **Analysing** involves demonstrating an ability to break a topic into its component parts and show the relationship between those parts by comparing and contrasting. How does x affect or relate to y. What piece of x or y is missing or could be seen to be needed?
- **Evaluating** involves a justification or an appraisal. For example, you could judge x according to a given criteria.
- **Creation** involves question verbs to design, construct, develop, formulate and imagine. Ultimately you are synthesising ideas or combining ideas or styles to formulate a new idea and to discuss how the application of these ideas will transform your professional practice and clinical settings.

Activity: Consider Bloom's knowledge levels and how they might be useful in the development of your professional practice and how you might utilise this model to demonstrate your knowledge and understanding in your writing?

For example, if we apply Blooms Taxonomy to the development of your leadership practice – how will you look when coaching your team members? Arguably goal-orientated coaching conversations are useful with your team members. This can be facilitated by taking a structured approach in which you ask questions that enable the team to better remember, understand, analyse, evaluate and synthesise a problem situation and to translate this into a goal they want to achieve and apply to bring about new ways of doing things. This is using Bloom's taxonomy in action.

Academic writing and enquiry are essentially about demonstrating your critical thinking ability and engagement with fresh ideas as summarised below:

- **Critical engagement** is about engaging with what you read; to interpret, analyse, evaluate and explain a subject area. We achieve this by developing a critical mindset and by asking searching questions of everything we read.

- **Critical thinking** is concerned with how we understand others work, evaluate other people's work, put together our own claims and link ideas in our argument. Critical thinking is not a singular skill but a combination of competencies that are required for success at university.

So how do we begin to engage critically with the work we are reading and researching?

Read widely and continually question what you are reading by asking why?

A depth of reading leads to a broad knowledge base where you need to critically engage with the material presented.

The academic process requires us to demonstrate an ability to consider different points of view and to deliver a rational and objective judgement of our ideas.

Developing our critical thinking suggests the deepening of our knowledge, skills and attitudes leading to new and innovative perspectives. Indeed Dewey (1910), in *How we think,* described critical thinking as reflective thinking that is active, persistent and carefully considers knowledge and beliefs to reach conclusions (Dewey, 1910, cited in McGregor, 2011). Cottrell (2005) describes critical thinking as a 'complex process of deliberation' which involves a wide range of skills and attitudes.

Arguably, the aim above all is to become proficient in *independent thinking* and advanced learning to develop a more sophisticated style of reasoning and a vision for better practice.

Our work needs to ask questions to develop fresh ideas. We need to add ideas to a discussion that until now may not have been considered.

Top Tip: The writer as a thinker, questions the information provided to illustrate solutions or fresh approaches.

Creating Arguments

In making arguments we define new ideas in a fresh and visionary way.

Arguments need to appear cohesive and inspiring and links directly to our practice; how we formulate our ideas and apply what we know is crucial.

Practice is defined in terms of the highest values and quality possible. Care practice is reviewed and needs to be re-examined in terms of the beliefs, values and attitudes that aim to enhance care delivery. People need to be viewed as individuals each with their own cultural identity and cared for by meeting their own individual needs.

Healthcare delivery needs to be understood as a partnership with best standards of care. Ultimately the way we think, defines what we do and how we do it. This leads us to look our approach and arguably there is significant value in being critically reflective in your approach. . .

Reflective practice is the ability to critically reflect on one's actions with the aim of making adaptations and learning. Reflecting in and on practice has huge benefits in increasing self-awareness, enhancing Professional Practice, of building emotional intelligence and in understanding others. Reflective practice supports the development of creative and critical thinking and develops active engagement in the workplace (Schon, 1993).

Thinking about situations that happen in our lives is a very human experience. However, reflective practice requires a conscious and active intention to think about events and to develop a deeper insight into them. Reflective practice is intertwined with experiential learning. Argyris (1993) argues that by stepping out of the single loop of experience and reflecting and conceptualising develops into a double loop of the reframing of ideas and enabling a paradigm shift to enable you to change what you do.

Reflective practice is an active, dynamic action-based and ethical set of skills, placed in real time and dealing with real, complex and difficult situations (Argyris, 1993).

Activity: Consider the following statements – what do they mean to you?
Effective reflection is a key tool in developing your academic writing and practice.
Effective reflection can allow professional practice to be enhanced.
Effective reflection is a process that can enable improvements in practice.
Effective reflection enables training or support needs to be identified.
Effective reflection supports effective practice to be shared.

The Value of Reflective Practice and Critical Thinking to Enhancing Your Writing and Clinical Practice

In clinical practice, the nurse, nursing associate, midwife, paramedic and indeed all health professionals are required to use precision and judgement 'to do the right thing, in the right way at the right time' (Odell, 2015).

In nursing, leadership and the allied health professions, it is important that we can demonstrate the rationale for our practice. Indeed in 2018, the National Medical Council (NMC) published its revised code of practice standards for the UK registered nurses and midwives and placed a significant emphasis in reasoning (NMC, 2018). The code outlines four areas of professional responsibility:

- *To prioritise people* – to attend to people considerately, respectfully and compassionately to healthcare service users and colleagues in practice. Arguably if you are to prioritise people it is important that you learn to think critically about the patient's situation and needs. You will need to observe patterns of behaviour and clinical presentations and ask key questions to assimilate and evaluate the information to enhance care delivery.
- *To practice effectively* – time and resources need to be utilised optimally. The code requires us to utilise evidence, to communicate clearly and work collaboratively with others. Clear and accurate records of care are important and when tasks are delegated to others we need to be assured of our accountability. Critical thinking enables us to consider what works best and why? Using evidence effectively enables us to recommend a best course of action for patients and by reflecting this with our patients we can then determine best practice in collaboration.

To preserve safety – the code requires nurses and midwives to work within the limits of their competence and the protocols and policies established within organisations that deliver healthcare. It is vital to raise concerns when patients are at risk, arguably we need to be able to quickly reflect on situations to deliver best practice and mitigate risk. Therefore, it is important that as practitioners we understand the limits of our competence, to be able to judge what we know and to think and reflect critically as safe practice can be demonstrated when we judge whether to act or not to act. Critical thinking and reflection are important in making better and safer decisions.

To promote professionalism and trust – The NMC Code (2018) outlines how Nurse has a professional responsibility to uphold the reputation of the profession and their own Nursing status. Leadership skills are required to promote the health and well-being of patients and the effectiveness of care delivery. Continuing Professional Development and learning is an ongoing process for the enhancement of care. By mastering new knowledge and the latest evidence we are instrumental in enhancing practice (NMC, 2018).

Action: Check out the latest guidance from your own Professional Body. It is important to be up to date.

Given the knowledge base and our professional body requirements, it is vital that as healthcare professionals we continuously develop our knowledge, practice, skills and critical thinking abilities to align our practice with the latest evidence and requirements.

Arguably 'decision-making, leadership and ethical practice are founded on an ability to think critically' (Price & Harrington, 2019). Critical thinking is a process that enables us to select relevant resources, to impart knowledge and evaluate evidence for its value and importance in clinical practice. As humans we develop our understanding through life in a tactic way, perhaps without any significant depth of thought. Critical thinking requires a more conscious level thinking. We are required to develop a deeper level of emotional and cognitive understanding.

Lovatt (2014) highlights critical thinking as 'a process, where different information is gathered, sifted, synthesised and evaluated, in order to understand a subject or issue'. Critical thinking engages our intellect (the ability to discriminate and argue), but it might engage our emotions too. To think critically we need to take account of values, beliefs and attitudes that shape our perceptions. Critical thinking then is that which the Nurse needs to function as a knowledgeable doer – someone who selects, combines, judges and uses information in order to proceed in a professional manner. Critical thinking is vital if we want to act strategically and to convey our care and compassion for others.

In the academic context, 'critical' has several different meanings (Morrall & Goodman, 2013). You may be asked to 'critically evaluate', 'to critically discuss' or 'critically explore' and this will vary according to the assessment criteria involved.

You may need to distinguish between right and wrong, make judgements about what is prominent or significant. However, a reflective piece the 'critical' component will involve you being introspective and self-aware.

The term 'critical thinking' requires us to develop the ability to analyse information, investigate it, to judge what might be relevant and to make decisions on what might be the most helpful. *Above all the aim is to make us more sensitive, imaginative and innovative in our practice.* Essentially when we apply critical thinking to practice, we need to explain the reasons why you have chosen the course of action you have and explain how it relates to key evidence that has influenced your practice.

Check point: As an example: if we examine the correct procedure for undertaking aseptic technique – how do we know how to do this? What does the evidence tell us about the correct course of action? We need to relate and embed our care practice with an understanding of evidenced-based practice to ensure quality, up-to-date evidence-based practice.
Check point: Can reflective models be of support to the process of critical self-reflection?

Reflective models of practice are extremely useful to enhance, extend and develop your professional practice in nursing, midwifery and allied health professions; and in developing personally with a level of emotional intelligence, the ability to be aware of, control and express one's emotions and to manage interpersonal relationships empathetically. According to Daniel Goleman et al. (2006), there are five main elements of emotional intelligence, self-awareness, self-regulation, motivation, empathy and social skills. Goleman et al. (2006) aim to develop your practice and to support you in becoming the best practitioner you can be by reflecting on situations and applying this new knowledge effectively in the future (more on this later).

Reflective practice is the ability to reflect on one's actions, so as to take a critical stance or attitude towards one's practice and engaging in a process of continuous adaptation and learning.

Developing reflective practice is arguably essential to those professions working with others and has become highly significant tool used in nursing, midwifery and paramedic practice. There is a key importance in developing accountability, supporting and verifying ability and noticing progression. As a critical process it enables personal and professional development and an increased self-awareness in relation to others. Ultimately reflective practice supports innovations in practice and enhances your confidence and enables you to articulate your ideas in your writing with further clarity. Reflective practice shifts your perspective, your lens is altered and new perspectives have the potential to emerge.

Let us review a few models to see what insights they might hold and make your selection to develop your practice. Figure 2.4 shows a version of Borton's model (1970) as developed further by John Driscoll in 2007.

What?	So What?	Now What?
This is the *description* and *self awareness* level and all questions start with the word what	This is the level of *analysis* and evaluation when we look deeper at what was behind the experience.	This is the level of *synthesis*. Here we build on the previous levels these questions to enable us to consider alternative courses of action and choose what we are going to do next.
Examples	**Examples**	**Examples**
What happened? What did I do? What did others do? What was I trying to achieve? What was good or bad about the experiences?	So what is the importance of this? So what more do I need to know about this? So what have I learnt about this?	Now what could I do? Now what do I need to do? Now what might I do? Now what might be the consequences of this action?

Figure 2.4   Borton's Model (1970)

Borton's Developmental framework is a straightforward and easy to implement reflective framework. It enables individual reflection without having the framework to hand and is recommended by many professional bodies and used by many universities. Its appeal lies in its three questions.

Activity: Review this model and consider if it might be useful to enhance your reflective practice?

Willis' Model is particularly helpful as it encourages the practitioner to engage with supportive literature whilst reflecting and apply this to practice in a tangible way. This clearly encourages a high degree of evidence-based practice, which is commendable (Figure 2.5).

Activity: Review Willis' Model (available here: https://jmvh.org/article/incor-porating-reflective-practice-as-an-assessment-tool-in-the-training-of-new-zealand-defence-force-nzdf-medics/) and consider if this model might be useful to enhance your reflective practice?

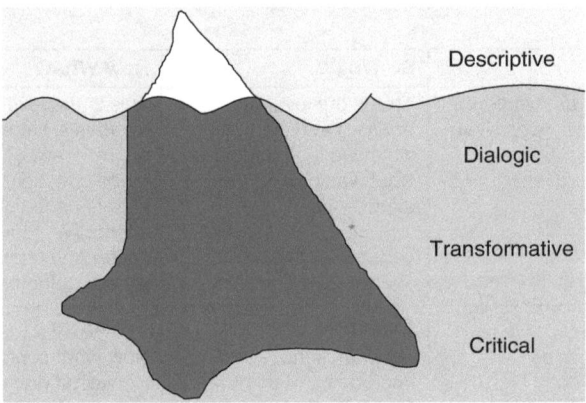

Figure 2.5 Nguyen Nhat Quang's Iceberg of Reflection 2022

Nguyen Nhat Quang's iceberg of reflection (2022) argues that reflection is not linear and adopts Flecks' (2012) classification into an iceberg of reflection, acknowledging that reflection consists of many layers and four stages.

Descriptive reflection is indicated as the tip of the iceberg, with narratives that do not represent the full picture to alter perspectives.

Dialogic reflection, just below the surface layer represents the interdependence and correlations of experience, through self-questioning and this self-questioning has the potential find alternative interpretations.

Transformative reflective enables a revisiting of the experience to create a more enabling process of growth.

Critical reflection is the deepest level of reflection and extends beyond the on-action reflection by looking at what, why and how through a holistic and ecological lens of social, historical, political and cultural factors.

The key focus on critical self-reflection lies in the reflector's metacognitive ability and sociocultural background (Figure 2.6).

Level	Stage	Questions to get you started
1	**Reporting and Responding**	Report what happened or what the issue or incident involved. Why is it relevant? Respond to the incident or issue by making observations, expressing your opinion, or asking questions.
2	**Relating**	Relate or make a connection between the incident or issue and your own skills, professional experience, or discipline knowledge. Have I seen this before? Were the conditions the same or different? Do I have the skills and knowledge to deal with this? Explain.
3	**Reasoning**	Highlight in detail significant factors underlying the incident or issue. Explain and show why they are important to an understanding of the incident or issue. Refer to relevant theory and literature to support your reasoning. Consider different perspectives. How would a knowledgeable person perceive/handle this? What are the ethics involved?
4	**Reconstructing**	Reframe or reconstruct future practice or professional understanding. How would I deal with this next time? What might work and why? Are there different options? What might happen if...? Are my ideas supported by theory? Can I make changes to benefit others?

Figure 2.6 Reflective Questions to Get You Started

The Advanced Model

This is designed by myself in support of advancing clinical practice and professional development, to include a focus on developing your knowledge, understanding, practice performance and behaviours.

The Advanced Model is a self-reflective model that supports critical appraisal and the development of knowledge, understanding, practice performance and professional behaviours for nursing practice and those allied to the healthcare professions using two examples of person-centred care and in working autonomously. You can apply this to various proficiencies that you are required to carry out throughout your practice.

Advance supports you towards independent practice and in meeting the standards for Health and Care Professional Council (HCPC) and NMC registration. This model is also advocated if you are required to develop a final year portfolio of evidence, in preparing for end-point interviews and in your ongoing professional development and in enhancing your critical appraisal skills.

The key element of this model lies in its ability to support you in demonstrating professional practice that is person-centred, evidence-based and mindful of the four patterns of nursing knowledge required for professional nursing practice including personal, empirical, ethical and aesthetic knowing (Chinn et al., 2015).

This will be useful for developing your critical writing, in providing feedback at your end-point assessments and in your ongoing professional development and advancing your patient care.

The Advanced Method uses key questions cited around the themes of practice performance, professional behaviour and knowledge and understanding used for almost any practice scenario that you wish to reflect upon.

Please review and consider the following Advanced Model questions in relation to Planning Care:

Practice Performance (Planning Care): What You Did

- Describe a situation and how you delivered it?
- How did you adapt your practice as it emerged in this situation?
- How did you demonstrate safety, proficiency and confidence practice?
- What were the boundaries of your practice in this situation?
- Did you seek support from a colleague and gain appropriate advice as required?
- How did you demonstrate leadership, delegation, supervision and challenge where necessary in this situation?

Practice Behaviour (Planning Care): How You Delivered It

- How did you demonstrate effective planning in your care practice?
- How did you give the coherent, accurate and necessary information to your patient?
- How did you ensure that your interventions and behaviour are both suitable and adaptable to the range of service users' circumstances?
- How did you identify and make appropriate referrals with the multidisciplinary team?
- How can you demonstrate your role in the effective working of the multidisciplinary team?
- How will you seek to develop your practice and that of others that promotes and sustains change?

Knowledge and Understanding (Planning Care): What Underpinned It

- What does the latest evidence say in support of your practice in this situation, demonstrate your understanding and delivery?
- How did you apply relevant evidence-based knowledge in this scenario?
- How can you demonstrate that your actions and communications held sound judgement?
- Can you critically analyse and demonstrate a range of alternative approaches that you have demonstrated in this situation?
- How do you develop your own and others practice that promotes and sustains change?
- In this scenario how do you self-reflect in and on your practice to critically evaluate the interventions used to inform and enhance your practice now and, in the future, to enhance your practice?

Please review and consider the following Advanced Method questions in relation to timely patient-centred care.

Practice Performance (Person-Centred Care): What You Did

- Describe a situation and how you prioritised and delivered timely person-centred effective care?
- How did you adapt your practice to the current and emerging situations in working with your patient?
- In this situation, how could you demonstrate that you were a safe, proficient and confident practitioner?
- Can you illustrate how you knew the boundaries of your practice in this situation?
- Did you require support and if so, how did you seek this out with a colleague and gain appropriate advice when needed?
- If required, how did you effectively lead, delegate, supervise and challenge in the given situation?

Professional Behaviour (Person-Centred Care): How You Delivered It

- How did you demonstrate careful and deliberate planning of person-centred care? Was this underpinned by a model of practice?
- How did you give coherent, accurate and necessary information to the patient?

- How did you ensure that your interventions and behaviour are both suitable and adaptable to the range of service users' circumstances?
- How did you identify and make appropriate referrals with the multidisciplinary team?
- How can you demonstrate your role in the effective working of the multidisciplinary team?
- How will you seek to develop your practice and that of others that promotes and sustains change?

Knowledge and Understanding (Person-Centred Care): What Underpinned It

- What does the latest evidence say in support of your practice in this situation, demonstrate your understanding and delivery of patient-centred care?
- How did you apply relevant evidence-based knowledge in this scenario?
- How can you demonstrate that your actions and communications held sound judgement in support of patient-centred care?
- Can you critically analyse and demonstrate a range of alternative approaches that you have demonstrated in this situation?
- How do you develop your own and others practice that promotes and sustains change?
- In this scenario, how do you self-reflect in and on your practice to critically evaluate the interventions used to inform and enhance your practice now and in the future to enhance your patient-centred practice?
- How do you demonstrate that you work autonomously, confidently and in partnership with people, their families and carers to ensure that their needs are met through care planning and delivery, including strategies for self-care and peer support.

Please review and consider the following Advanced Model questions in relation to the themes of safe, competent and confident practice.

Practice Performance (Safe, Competent and Confident Practice): What You Did

- Describe a situation that addresses the proficiency of demonstrating how you work autonomously, with confidence and in partnership to deliver care excellence in working autonomously, confidently and in partnership?

- How did you in this scenario adapt your practice to current and emerging situations?
- In this situation you describe, how could you demonstrate that you were a safe, proficient and confident practitioner in working autonomously, confidently and in partnership?
- Can you illustrate how you knew the boundaries of your practice in this situation in working autonomously, confidently and in partnership?
- Did you require support to fulfil the proficiency and if so, how did you seek this out with a colleague and gain appropriate advice when needed to demonstrate how you worked autonomously, confidently and in partnership?
- Can you cite a situation relating to the proficiency where you demonstrate how you effectively lead, delegate, supervise and challenge in the given situation to demonstrate how you worked autonomously, confidently and in partnership?

Professional Behaviour (Safe, Competent and Confident Practice): How You Delivered It

- In this scenario, how did you demonstrate careful and deliberate planning of person-centred care to demonstrate how you worked autonomously, confidently and in partnership? In this scenario, how did you give coherent, accurate and necessary information to the patient demonstrating how you worked autonomously, confidently and in partnership?
- In this scenario, how did you ensure that your interventions and behaviour are both suitable and adaptable to the range of service users' circumstances demonstrating how you worked autonomously, confidently and in partnership?
- In this scenario, how did you identify and make appropriate referrals with the multidisciplinary team demonstrating how you worked autonomously, confidently and in partnership?
- In this scenario, how can you demonstrate your role in the effective working of the multidisciplinary team demonstrating how you worked autonomously, confidently and in partnership?

Knowledge and Understanding (Safe, Competent and Confident Practice): What Underpinned It

- What does the latest evidence say in support of your practice in this situation, demonstrating how you worked autonomously, confidently and in partnership? How can you demonstrate how your practice should seek to deliver autonomous, confident practice that works in support of your patient and their families and patient needs and in the promotion of self-care and peer support?

- How did you apply relevant evidence-based knowledge in this scenario demonstrating how you worked autonomously, confidently and in partnership?
- In the scenario you raise, how can you demonstrate that your actions and communications held sound judgement in support of autonomous, confident practice that worked with your patient and their families in support of patient needs and in the promotion of self-care and peer support?
- Can you critically analyse and demonstrate a range of alternative approaches that you have demonstrated in this situation? In demonstrating autonomous, confident practice in support of patient care how would you enhance your practice in a similar situation?
- Having cited this example, how would you in future develop your own and others practice that promotes and sustains change?
- In this scenario, how do you self-reflect in and on your practice to critically evaluate the interventions used to inform and enhance your practice now and in the future?

Question: How has this model and the depth of questions enabled you to self-reflect and critically appraise your practice?

Action: Apply any scenario that has been a recent event at work to the questions above to demonstrate your knowledge and understanding and professional performance

Top Tip: Above all we need to remember that reflection aims to develop a deep understanding and depth of knowledge and an opportunity to apply our critical thinking, with the aim of enhancing innovating within our practice.

Activity: Review the models, research others or be guided by your Higher Education Institute and consider which model might be useful to enhance your reflective practice.

Remember academic argument must be based on factual information, previous theoretical claims. Have you gathered all the information required to formulate your arguments? Remember that critical thinking involves not considering any view as 'truth' but by considering if you are being objective. Continually and proactively ask questions.

Check point: Critical evaluation is about applying and justifying our positions and demonstrating this in our writing to enhance innovation in practice with factual evidence. It is important to consider this in the planning of your discussion points. How will you plan to achieve this going forward. What tools will you use? (More on this later.)

3
Planning for Academic Writing

Key Points

Together in Chapter 3, we will examine and explore the following themes:

- The value of reading and researching ideas.
- Reading for enhanced critical thinking – how we develop this.
- How to source and evaluate literature.
- Develop your critical thinking skills.
- Effectively evaluate your chosen sources.

The Value of Reading and Researching Ideas

Research acts to develop and deepen your knowledge of the subject and the systematic process of learning.

Your programme will require you to write in various formats and demonstrate your understanding from a variety of sources, not just your own ideas. Use of these sources supports your evidence and demonstrates your ability to understand the wider picture.

Top Tip: Ensure you are crystal clear on what your assignment/assessment is requiring you to do. Look at the keywords embedded in the programme and source key literature that adds to you building a rich picture for you to discuss, explore, analyse and evaluate from.

Reading Widely Enables You to Develop Your Writing

A depth of reading around your subject area is key to your academic success. By engaging in wide reading around the subject area and listening reflecting, noting the theoretical positions and views of others we assimilate ideas and develop a depth of understanding of our subject area and can then seek to scaffold and build our knowledge as we have discussed earlier when referring to Blooms Taxonomy. This has the potential to lead to new opinions and to develop our practice.

Check point: Please note usual academic practice cites ten high-quality references for every 1,000 words.

Developing Skills for Effective Reading

As a reminder here as you will know this of course, but the purpose is to gather information to form your discussion points, so the first question to ask is: does the text provide the relevant information you require? Your reading needs to be for a reason, relevant to the task and active, whereby you construct the meaning of the texts you are reviewing. Remember too, it is important to read with a critical mindset that seeks to evaluate the lines of argument in the texts, to deconstruct fact from ideas so that you can objectively reach a conclusion to your questions.

Check points: it is important to consider:

- Relevant reading
- Active reading
- How you develop a critical mindset around the ideas you are reading
- Examine the structure and patterns in the whole picture of the works you are examining.

The importance of reading widely adds to the currency and robustness of your work. What we want to achieve is a depth of learning within a subject area, to build new knowledge and to enhance the application of theoretical principles to our practice experience. Reading widely may begin with material you have collated in the form of lecture and tutorial notes. From there, it is important to be proactive in accessing libraries and recommended leading lists. Textbooks (physical or eBooks), journals, research articles, policy documents and national guidelines are all important sources for nursing and healthcare studies.

> **Top Tip:** Universities often have library specialists who are highly knowledgeable in their field, so you are advised to access them as a key resource. **Check point:** how do you plan to collate your ideas to build on your work and formulate your ideas over time? Endnote and Onenote are really useful tools. Again your professional advisors within your university libraries can guide you.

Developing Reading for Enhanced Critical Thinking – How We Develop This?

Critical thinking is the process of carefully and systematically examining research to judge its trustworthiness, value and relevance in a particular context.

The application of critical thinking to our work is demonstrated by our ability to interpret, analyse, evaluate and explain the value and relevance of ideas to a particular context (Burls 2009).

> **Top Tip:** Ask questions of all that you read and carefully consider how the ideas can translate into enhancing practice.

Application – Why Is Critical Thinking Useful?

Critical thinking is useful in our everyday lives and within the world of work as it facilitates our ability to make informed decisions with depth and understanding and to develop what we do in innovative ways.

> **Check point:** How could you develop your critical thinking skills, what activities could you undertake?
> **Top Tip:** Find your buddy.

With my own students I have often suggested a buddy system – where you identify a colleague and work together to review and edit each other's work and ideas and to stretch each other in your learning via the materials you are reviewing. It enables you to consider your ideas more fully.

How to Source and Evaluate Literature

The criteria for evaluation (relevance, accuracy, authority, purpose and timeliness) – use the acronym TRAPP.

Consider the following of what you read:

Keywords are the ideas within a title and will form the key search phrases. Synonyms or alternative key words are important to consider to set the parameters of your research strategy.

- Author's purpose
- Tone and ideas of the authors
- Analyse – the strengths and weaknesses of the ideas
- Evaluate – how these ideas are useful to enhance and innovate practice if applied

If you are new to research and literature searching, all colleges and higher education providers have study skills and online database courses that you can access. The libraries offer excellent resources with highly knowledgeable staff and training.

More on these themes later on.

> **Top Tip:** Complete the literature search before you begin writing and consider each piece's relevance thoroughly. This involves asking key questions around the validity and reliability of the research you are reading when formulating your ideas.

Check point:
- **Validity** means that a tool measures what its sets out to measure, for example that a pain assessment tools measures pain intensity rather than anxiety.
- **Reliability** refers to the consistency, stability and repeatability of results. Testing for reliability ensures that the consistent results would be obtained in identical situations on different occasions. Interestingly a measure can be reliable but not valid.

Action point: It is important to consider the validity or legitimacy of the literature that you read and review. How will you look to embed this into your practice?
Top Tip: Use a critical evaluation tool.

The importance of critical appraisal tools is acknowledged but there is no consensus on a gold standard tool (Katrak et al., 2004).

Check point: Please check with your lecturer on the required tool that your Institution prefers and recommends.

With the volume of online information, a useful free resource is the Critical Appraisal Skills Programme (CASP) www.casp-uk.net which offers for free appraisal tools for different methods including.

- Systematic review checklist
- RCT checklists
- Case control study checklists
- Diagnostic checklists
- Economic evaluation checklists
- Clinical prediction rule checklists
- Qualitative research checklists

Top Tip: Using Evernote or EndNote is a great way to capture and track your ideas.

4

Examining Different Writing Styles for Different Purposes

Key Points

Together in Chapter 4, we will examine and explore the following themes:

- Examine different writing styles.
- Understand the distinction of working between writing in the personal/subjective reflection and critical reflection.
- Identify the requirements of essay, report, personal and reflective writing.
- Identify key sources to support your writing skills.

Academic Writing Under the Microscope

There is an expectation in academic writing that you produce ideas that are logically structured, well argued and proven ideas that take account of differing opinions. Regardless of the style you are writing in, your work needs to be accurate, formal, direct and concise. You need to develop a sense of authority, with accurately referenced ideas.

Academic styles of writing are generally objective, rather than personal. Generally, avoid the use of I, you and me. The use of impersonal language is key, for example the only place for emotive language in academic writing is within reflective writing. More on this later. Use of questions and contracted words (such as don't, can't and shouldn't) should be reserved for oral presentations and not within academic writing.

Academic Writing Style Requirements

Your assessments will fall under various guises of writing. Let us take a look at some examples:

Reflective Writing: Involves looking back at something and explaining/ analysing from different perspectives. Various models of reflective writing are available.

Reflective writing demands your opinion and gives you the freedom to express this. The use of 'I' is permitted.

Reflective writing in academic terms still requires you to produce writing that delivers a depth of understanding and analysis and follows a systematic and step-by-step approach.

Reflective writing must use your experience in support of your ideas, it needs to explore the implications and outcomes of actions taken and consider various perspectives on the ideas you raise.

The Power of Asking *Why* Holds Great Significance

It is useful to you as a student to develop your learning approach and to form your longer term goals.

Reflective practice is used as an assessment tool in universities to develop the student's ability to think critically and to solve problems.

It also holds value in life skills and develops an inner process of thinking about our actions and the consequences of these in daily life.

Ultimately by reflecting on events or ideas we can witness personal and professional development and how we make sense of them.

Remember the learning cycle and how you will apply this. Learning from experience is often known as the learning cycle and refers to the work undertaken by Kolb (1984).

How do you demonstrate your learning from practice?

Check point: When marking reflective writing pieces, as lecturers we are looking for certain criteria within the work. The following questions are useful for you to consider when you write your next reflective piece as follows:

- Does your work consider the uncertainty of practice?
- Do you consider the consequences of your actions?
- Do you think about change and change management?
- Do you explore one or two events in depth?
- Do you relate the events to your own personal development?

Check point: As we have identified, your reflective writing needs to hold depth, analysis and structure. One way of achieving this is to use a reflective model. There are many available to use and your academic institution may specify a preferred model as a reflective learning cycle. Action: Please review Chapter 1 to review and select your critical model for reflection on and in practice.

Report writing: uses explanatory language and a structure to persuade with the aim of approving or disproving a hypothesis.

A report usually follows an event or research. For example an annual or survey report. It will hold key headings:

- Part 1: An outline of the work and a summary of findings.
- Part 2: Sections indicating the development of the findings.
- Part 3: References, appendices and bibliography.

Essay writing: the essay and report cover all disciplines. Structure is key and involves exploring an area in depth. The essay is used as a tool to explore an area in detail. For example the importance, value or impact of a certain theory.

You are usually expected to offer your point of view on the subject area.

The essay title will hold key direction words that guide your style and direction, for example Discuss, Explain or Outline.

Ethical writing: Acknowledging another's work.

Discursive writing: This involves persuasive writing where the author argues strongly for or against a given viewpoint. In argumentative writing opposing viewpoints are outlined in a more balanced way which aims to examine a range of ideas. A balanced discussion requires you write objectively in a written formal style. Report writing is an example.

Persuasive writing: Your argument informs your point of view/aims to persuade.

> **Check point:** In the planning phase, we need to consider the requirements of the assignment you need to complete. This will vary according to the writing style and the key words specified in your assignment brief (Gillet et al., 2009).
>
> **Top Tip:** It sounds so simple but frequently students fail to clearly understand and apply the knowledge required to the brief. A top tip is to check your assignments key words and the marking criteria. Select the keywords, give meaning to them and consider how you will action what is required.

5

Developing Your Critical Writing Skills and Structuring Critical Argument

Key Points

Together in Chapter 5, we will examine the next crucial step in the academic writing process by examining:

- What academic writing requires and developing a process of enquiry.
- The importance of critical thinking and creating arguments – weighing it all up.
- How to give clarity to the ideas you present via your choice of key words.
- Examining frameworks for creating and deconstructing argument and enhancing your critical thinking skills.
- The application of critical writing and how to effectively structure your work and robustly articulate your arguments with check points and examples.
- Carefully selecting keywords to demonstrate your ideas definitively.

Academic writing is formal in nature and needs to meet the required standards of the programme you are studying. Your work is assessed in terms of its quality against these standards.

There is an expectation in academic writing that you produce ideas that are logically structured, well argued and proven ideas that take account of differing opinions.

Regardless of the style you are writing in, your work needs to be accurate, formal, direct and concise.

It needs to offer a sense of authority with accurately referenced ideas.

Writing the perfect piece is like drawing the perfect circle. Meaning that no matter what you do you'll always end up with a zero? Not meaning it's impossible, but with the right tools, you can get pretty darn close.

Let Us Look at an Initial Process for Building Your Ideas – Stages 1–8

If you find developing structure in your assignment challenging or knowing a clear process of building your work you may wish to consider an eight-stage approach to building critical appraisal skills in our writing developed by the author:

- **Stage 1:** Explore the evidence: following your literature review, identify other people's positions, lines of argument and conclusions.
- **Stage 2:** Using a critical review framework (The Critical Appraisal Skills Programme (CASP) Tool is useful, www.casp-uk.net) evaluate the evidence by weighing up opposing arguments and evidence, read between the lines and identify false or biased assumptions.
- **Stage 3:** Examine the bias of opinion and the use of persuasive techniques.
- **Stage 4:** Reflect on issues in a structured way, bringing logic and insight to the forefront of your discussion points.
- **Stage 5:** Draw conclusions about the validity and reliability and justifiability of arguments based on good evidence and supportive ideas.
- **Stage 6:** In academic writing we need to consider if we have explored the whole picture and not just one point of view.
- **Stage 7:** Present your points in a structured, clear and convincing format that appears rational, i.e. we need to identify the reasons for what we believe and do and consider other people's reasoning.

- **Stage 8:** Importantly we need to reach conclusions on what we have read, to voice our opinion and look at the impact of knowledge and ideas for practice.

Critical Writing and Creating Arguments – Weighing It All Up!

It is important to remember that an argument takes a particular stand on an issue and provides evidence to back it up. A key point to understand in academic writing is that it has a main argument running through it. This is created by our wide reading of the subject area under study. At university level, this is combined with critical thinking, the ability to engage with other people's arguments and form arguments of your own. It is therefore important to consider what argument actually looks like. An argument has at least one reason, it attempts to persuade the reader and it has a conclusion. Argument must be based on factual information, previous theoretical claims, questioning all views as truth, being objective and asking questions. Critical evaluation is about applying, justifying and discussing the evidence that supports it. To critically engage with the argument, you need to make a judgement and assess the validity of it.

Activity: Identify the argument in the following statement and consider the reliability of the evidence.

The majority of people do not smoke. Passive smoking can cause ill health. Therefore people should not be allowed to smoke in public places.

The argument is this statement proposes that people should not be allowed to smoke in public places. However, the supporting evidence is vague.

The first sentence refers to the majority of people not smoking, but does not quantify or qualify this. Neither the first nor second sentences base their claims on solid evidence.

What is the evidence that passive smoking causes ill health and what ill health does it cause? How many are affected?

Be specific, focused and clear. It is also evident that this argument does not engage with alternative perspectives such as those who argue that smoking in public places is an issue of personal freedom. It is important to consider all angles in the argument.

Top Tip: To enhance your writing extend the range of your reasoning and limit the range of the conclusion.

Points for Creating and Deconstructing Argument and Enhancing Your Critical Thinking Skills

1 What is the context and why is it important?
2 Consider the issues thoroughly from different perspectives.
3 Are there alternative arguments or explanations that need considering?
4 What exactly is the author arguing?
5 Evaluate the evidence, put forward in support of the viewpoint – is the argument logical?
6 Does the evidence support the argument fully or partially?
7 What are the measurable or observable facts?
8 How strong is the evidence?
9 How big is the sample – is it representative enough?
10 Is the source reputable and unbiased?
11 What is quoted from other sources?
12 What is implicitly or explicitly assumed to be true without any support?
13 Are there alternative arguments or explanations?
14 What is the main conclusion or recommendation?
15 Check whether the conclusions are rational. If not, the viewpoint should be reconsidered.
16 What are the minor conclusions? Are they robust enough?
17 Consider the implications: What conclusions would follow?

The application of critical writing and how to effectively structure your work and robustly articulate your arguments, framework to consider.

Academic writing has been described as writing up the facts of the How, Who, What, Where and When. This has to develop and form an argument. There are several steps that you can take to make this easier.

Read and make notes from your sources and examine the principles and values of the research you are reviewing with key questions:

Is the work a valuable contribution to the field?
Is the work innovative? rigorous?
Look at the research criteria – Why, Where, How, When and with whom did the research take place?
What are the strengths and weaknesses of the work?

Does the work offer new insights?

Do quotes support the argument?

What are the implications and innovations for practice?

Developing a Structured Argument

Academic writing requires you to develop your argument and provide statements of what you think about the question you have been set. This lies at the heart of the academic process and needs to be demonstrated within your writing.

Being critical demonstrates your understanding of the issue and the strengths and weaknesses of it.

Your argument determines your structure, reasoning, quotations, introduction and conclusion. Spend time on it. The answer to the question ultimately comes from your reading and finding structured, logical and cohesive discussion points – there is no one single answer it depends on your findings.

Above all you are aiming to persuade your reader and everything in your writing should support your argument.

Top Tip: find a method that suits your approach.
Activity: Carefully take a look at the following frameworks, take some of your writing and restructure your ideas by following the frameworks below.

The Simple Model

(S1) Start by introducing the argument to the reader and its importance.

(S2) Indicate the reasons and evidence for the argument.

(S3) Discuss the reasons and evidence against the argument.

(S4) Summarise both points of view and discuss and explain your own viewpoint.

The Simple Model: Example A

An example of Level 7 writing demonstrating critical evaluation via an assessment in nursing practice.

Activity: Can you spot the fluidity of the writing style and the application (synthesis) of ideas?

(S1): There are various definitions of assessment, but in its application the assessment process acts as a robust and effective tool to ensure that a person is knowledgeable and competent in their role. Gopee (2015) suggests that assessment is a vital part of the mentor's role. Moreover, the purpose of assessment is to ensure that the learner fosters professional growth and develops the required knowledge, skills and attitudes for competency as a Professional Nurse (NMC, 2015). **(S2):** We are also reminded of the work of Duffy (2009) who indicates how we are 'failing to fail' within Nursing assessment. Of crucial importance is the validity and reliability of the assessment process. It requires the mentor to assess the link and application of theory to practice and give consistency and meaning to the use of evidence based practice. It should also underpin the Nursing and Midwifery Council (NMC) domains for Nurse registration. **(S3):** Walsh (2010) suggests that there is supportive evidence to propose that assessment is not a priority in clinical practice; although he argues that it should be. It is apparent that the mentor facilitates learning through providing constructive feedback and is accountable in validating the student's competency within the domains of learning which include the knowledge, skills and attitudes necessary for the role. **(S4):** In summary this evidence clearly indicates how the mentor is crucial in promoting leadership for learning and reinforces the importance of assessing the required knowledge, skills and attitudes that relate directly to the Professional Nursing role and the application of theory to practice (Walsh, 2010).

Simple Model: Example B

(S1) Research linked to effective leadership is presented in multi-faceted ways. Indeed, leadership efficacy can be viewed as holding a set of personality characteristics including a range of skills, traits, behaviours and attributes. Interestingly Northouse (2016) cites the importance of an effective leader as having the capacity to authentically influence others in the organisation, towards a set of organisational goals. The leader's ability to understand, set and build upon the strategic direction alongside the organisation's stakeholders can be viewed as a distinct organisational advantage. **(S2)** Covey (2004) discusses the underlying importance of the capacity of the visionary leader to both value and build organisational relationships across all levels of the organisation which leads to the development and progression of organisational strategic goals. Bryman (2007) identified 11 measures of higher education leadership, whereas Gibbs et al. (2009) developed nine key clusters and Kouzes and Posner (1998) five elements of effective leadership practice. Based on these findings, Parrish (2015) developed a Leadership Competency Framework consisting of five leadership practices assimilated from the three models and viewed as a set of practices that reflected sound, effective and applicable academic leadership competencies (see Appendix 2). **(S3)** Conversely ineffectual leadership that fails to execute the organisations mission negatively impacts organisational performance and team efficacy (Jones & Olken, 2005). **(S4)** If we connect these ideas with the rapid changes currently affecting Higher Education Institutions (HEIs) in the United Kingdom as indicated by Lumby (2012) 'as the perfect storm of external challenges and pressures', it is evident that proficient leadership competencies are required to deliver effective strategic change, organisational sustainability and growth (Prosci.com). There is an evident need to question the traditional boundaries in a university and to review 'an appropriate strategic stance' (Barnett, 2011; Brown & Carasso, 2013).

Advanced Method: Example A

The Advanced Method is a persuasive approach that uses your argument as the starting point and has been adapted for ease of use as follows:

- **(A1)** Start by introducing generally and express your discussion point.
- **(A2)** Explain your rational for the argument.
- **(A3)** Explain the reasons against the argument.
- **(A4)** Counter the reasons against the argument.
- **(A5)** Provide reasons for your argument, i.e. the case for your view with examples, evidence and explanation.
- **(A6)** Conclusion – restate your line of argument and the rationale for its importance.
- **(A7)** Apply this as required to your area of practice and identify new ways of working.

(A1) Student nurses have a unique role in supporting quality improvement (Open University (OU, 2022a)). Quality in healthcare is a complex concept, reflected in everything healthcare professionals do, say and think (OU, 2022b). **(A2)** Quality

Healthcare must be safe, effective, person-centred, timely, efficient and equitable (World Health Organisation, 2018 cited in OU, 2022b). Student nurses come to each practice learning environment with new eyes and have the opportunity to observe both good and poor practice to other areas (OU, 2022a). **(A3)** However, this experience can be complex and reveal the true realities of care within a challenged and overburdened healthcare system. **(A4)** During a placement it was evident that there was a need for a standardised approach to care, as cited in the National Institute for Health and Clinical Excellence (NICE, 2010) and it is apparent that an understanding of leadership theories, skills and approaches holds the potential to effectively lead service improvement initiatives and to facilitate this as a strategic leader (OU, 2022c). **(A5)** This depth of knowledge of leadership theories and approaches has great potential for both personal and professional development (Goleman, 2000). Primarily, it enables the healthcare practitioner to understand their own work context and to strategically consider how it is possible to lead service innovation both strategically and methodically by following a process of delivery. Similarly an understanding of leadership theories has the potential to enable the leader to identify their own leadership style; by examining various leadership theories, a leader can gain insight into their own natural tendencies and behaviours when leading a team. This self-awareness has the potential to support practitioners to leverage their strengths and work on areas of weakness (West et al., 2017). **(A6)** There is also the potential for key learning in adapting one's leadership style. Different situations may require different leadership styles, and understanding various theories can help a leader choose the best approach for a given situation. For example, a leader may need to use a more directive approach when dealing with a crisis, or a more participative approach when working with a team of highly skilled professionals. **(A7)** It is most apparent that to be an effective leader, it is important to hold an understanding of various approaches, styles, qualities and behaviours that can be used as tools in various contexts and situations. An enlightened leader has the awareness to understand that the key lies in agility and using the right approach at the right time (Francis, 2020). Apply this as required to your area of practice and identify new ways of working.

A 12-Point Approach to Writing

You may wish to consider a 12-point approach to writing as follows:

1 Question
2 Research

3   Point

4   Appraise

5   Rational

6   Evidence

7   Critical analysis

8   Critical Evaluation

9   Synthesis

10   Application

11   Professional Growth

12   Conclusion

Activity: Follow the 12-point approach illustrated in this example.

Here we evidence the 12 steps are indicated with bracketed numbers as follows:

A critical evaluation of the application of a strategic boundary spanning model to enhance the delivery of organisational strategic objectives within an HEI.

1   Whilst huge variations exist in the conceptualisation of effective leadership from the focus of leadership as a process, to leadership from a personality perspective, that involve a set of behaviours, skills and traits, the power relationships in existence, the capacity to influence others and a focus on working towards common goals (Northouse, 2016).

2   The most important competitive advantage of the organisation can be identified as effective leadership, in setting the strategic direction and in building its resources, namely its operations and employees. Jones and Olken (2005) and Covey (2004) identify how visionary leaders actively seek to communicate the worth of others to enable them to identify it within themselves indicating the value of organisational relationships.

3   In contrast, Jones and Olken (2005) illustrate how poor organisational leadership has an impact on organisational performance and

(Continued)

(Continued)

efficiency in teams and fails to execute the strategic vision and goals of the organisation. If we look at these ideas in connection with the 'perfect storm of external challenges and pressures' faced by the UK university sector, which Lumby discusses in 2012, it is clear that there are a number of current drivers for strategic change that require proficient leadership skills. Change management is useful in defining the methods, processes and tools to manage the people side of change, to achieve a desired result (Prosci, 2019).

4   The author set out to examine in detail the internal context of a known higher education institution (HEI) to examine its current issues and to critically analyse a planned change via a change model, conscious that internal issues could hinder the success of addressing the external challenges identified.

5   The initial research undertaken for this chapter involved questionnaires and in depth semi-structured interviews (see Appendix 1) with the senior management team. The questions examined leadership approaches, barriers and awareness of challenges facing the organisation and took into account that these positions would involve both internal and external engagement (see Appendix 1). Initial findings from interviews and in viewing communications identified a weakness in cross boundary collaboration with a culture of blame and a lack of collective decision-making evident from internal communications. It was also evident that the interviewees perceived significant constraints in their leadership activity both within internal and external peer-to-peer boundaries of function with staff working in isolation with significant challenges to building alliances and a lack of authentic stakeholder engagement. Similarly, the HEI under discussion did not seem to have an effective communication strategy to deliver its strategic plan; its internal relationships with stakeholders seemed weak, with a lack of collective decision-making and a leadership style that does not motivate and inspire.

6   With the identification of these micro issues, it is also important to examine the macro problems currently affecting HEIs to gain a complete picture. The government's removal of block subsidy for

student fees has led to a dependence on a market environment in securing courses and is of the utmost importance for financial success (Barnett, 2011; Clarke, 2004; Gibb et al., 2012, Shattock, 2009). This shifts the focus of the HEI towards 'entrepreneurial' leadership and strategies to ensure student recruitment, retention and satisfaction targets and is brought into sharper focus, especially with the United Kingdom's potential exit from the European Union and the current unknown implications of this for student recruitment and on research funding streams (Prysor & Henley, 2017). The introduction of the Teaching Excellence Framework has led to a lack of clarity on the shape of the UK HEI quality assurance framework and an increased focus on procedures for monitoring and compliance (Universities UK, 2015). Similarly, there is a focus amongst HEIs to nourish income streams internationally, with tighter regulation of student recruitment. The result has led to a number of new strategies to develop programme partnership and franchising opportunities for students and fee income.

7   These issues coupled with a requirement of HEIs to demonstrate research impact, to build 'entrepreneurial opportunities from knowledge transfer and exchange', (Prysor & Henley, 2017, p. 31) to demonstrate economic value to ensure student employability and to reshape traditional learning delivery models via massive open on-line courses (MOOCs) illustrate the pace and complexity of change within the HEI sector and requires salient and effective leadership skills. In relation to this complexity, Prysor and Henley (2017) identify the importance of addressing a perspective or paradigm shift leading from the management of processes to visionary leadership (Ramsden, 1998, p. 34) and the ability to understand and manage complexity (Seale & Cross, 2015), to build planning frameworks and skills (Stark et al., 2002) and to valuing leadership qualities that pertain to emotional intelligence, consideration of others and effective communication (Parish, 2015). Given the micro and macro issues identified, this chapter will seek to evaluate how an identified model has the potential to support the development of effective relationships, support the enhanced delivery of organisational objectives and to address the widening number of boundaries required in HEI.

(Continued)

(Continued)

8   The initial task was to choose a change management model that would support a depth of enquiry into the issues identified and an analysis of the situational problem. Hayes (2007) articulates the value models play in the defining issues of organisational behaviour that require attention. Kotter's Eight Steps (2012), Senge Systems Theory (2014) and Ernst & Chrobot-Mason's Boundary Spanning Model (2017) were examined for their usefulness and potential problem-solving capabilities within the given HEI as people and process models of change. Kotter clearly identifies the value and importance of change leadership in a rapidly changing world and that without it change falters and excellence becomes problematic (Kotter, 1996, p. 144).

9   Due to the level of discord and low staff morale in the known organisation and for its inclusive relational approach and specific focus on strategic leadership for HEIs, the author focused on the Boundary Spanning Model of Change (Ernst & Chrobot-Mason, 2011b) as the optimal choice to support the change process in this instance. This chapter postulates that the application of a strategic and boundary spanning model of leadership has the potential to address both the internal and external relational issues. The rational for the application of this change management framework will now be critically appraised.

10   Whilst commendable in theory, the successful application of this model may prove challenging to an existing senior management team (SMT). The implementation of the model requires a new leadership approach, which the SMT would need to recognise, value and embrace and would require key interpersonal skills, arguably a high level of emotional intelligence (Coleman, 2012; Yip et al., 2016) and the capability to engage with diversely positioned individuals in a common cause towards innovation and change. Within the delivery of the boundary spanning leadership (BSL) approach, feelings of threat and variations in individual perceptions can be difficult to overcome to reach transformation. The BSL model relies heavily on leaders as change agents with excellent leadership, communication, motivational and conflict resolution skills (Barrett, 2003; Prysor &

Henley, 2017). Leaders are also required to examine their own style of leadership. They need to monitor for personal bias and to assess the impact of their leadership on the vision, creativity and strategic alignment within an organisation and to assess the efficacy of their relationship with stakeholders. The process is time consuming and challenging work and requires the leader to welcome this level of self-reflection to bring about innovation and change (Johnson & Scholes, 1999; Prysor & Henley, 2017). However, it is vital for SMT to understand that a vision is only of value when true measurement can be qualified in terms of how it achieves the objectives of the organisation.

11 This chapter has outlined via three identified problem areas, how the application of a boundary spanning model and a symmetrical communications approach impacts on employee engagement in building of relationships, overcoming boundary constraints and ultimately to the successful implementation of strategic goals (Erikson, 2010; Gregory & Willis, 2009; Forsyth, 2010). The BSL model recognises how as employees, we are clearly affected by an organisation's decisions and effective leadership should encourage active engagement with its employees to support its mission (Grunig, 1992; Prysor & Henley, 2017; Steyn, 2005). Communication is crucial in mobilising and transforming durable relationships that organisations require for support and in valuing staff (Steyn, 2005). Nayab (2010) highlights how visionary leaders thrive to motivate people to a shared vision and 'communicate with team members'. Despite the time and the long-term investment required, an integrated approach to strategic management is crucial. It is evident within the BSL model that well-thought-out strategies, systems and behaviours that work authentically with stakeholders in considering their points of view, in building bridges and developing relationships through person–person linkages has a positive organisational impact and in valuing their contribution as stakeholders (James & Scholes, 2010).

12 In summary, it is indicative that effective leadership theory has transitioned from valuing highly directional leadership, based on

(Continued)

(Continued)

authority, power and influence (indeed criticised for being too black and white; Molero et al., 2007), towards a relationship management approach, that values a democratic, fair, authentic decision-making process and takes account of group dynamics and validates staff for their contribution (Ernst & Chrobot-Mason, 2011b; Prysor & Henley, 2017; Steyn, 2005). This chapter has indicated how BSL seeks to engage stakeholders, build collaborative, trust-based relationships, improve communication and drive the organisations vision and strategic objectives via a collective 'buy in'. This significantly relies on a leadership style that is inclusive, engaging and seeks to reach out to build relationships both internally and externally. The BSL model reinforces the importance of including all members of the organisation and within the change process. To effectively embed BSL leadership into the organisation under discussion the author has suggested that a significant investment in the constructive use of appraisal time could go a long way in demonstrating how staff are valued partners in the organisation. Similarly, the use of 'team time' activities could be an effective way to collaboratively discuss and clarify the organisations direction in line with its core objectives. This would be visionary BSL in action and holds the potential to proactively overcome the issues identified.

Action: Given the demonstration of several structural models for enhancing your writing – which one will you plan to assimilate into your work to construct and present your ideas. To extend your discussion points, link it to another idea and question it in depth. Ideas should never be left in isolation but link to your key themes an idea, with extension and flow throughout your work. What is your next step in achieving this in your writing?

Choosing Your Words

Your claims in your work need to be clear, strong, definitive and illustrate confidence in your position. You can give clarity to your ideas by being clear on your position, avoiding vast statements, using supporting evidence, linking ideas and acknowledging the ideas of others. Let us now consider some wording you might use to achieve this.

Words to Demonstrate a Comparison of Ideas

- However (can be used to identify alternative ideas)
- Similarly (identifies links)
- In contrast (signals an alternative)

Phrases to Critique

- This illustrates a limited understanding of...
- These claims are controversial because...
- The main shortcomings of this evidence appear to be...
- The key difficulty with this approach is identified within.
- This claim is problematic because...

Phrases to Make Your Position Clear

As we have discussed it is important for you to find a strong and definitive voice in your writing.

One tangible way of achieving this is to be very clear on the position you take in relation to the arguments you make, but delivered in a cautious manner with careful phrasing and by linking your ideas.

- It is possible that...
- It is clear that...
- By introducing these ideas, the effect may be...
- Perhaps this indicates.... the likelihood that...
- This research suggests...

Your choice of keywords is very helpful in defining the strength and tone of your argument. You may wish to consider some of the following phrases:

Positive Phrasing

- These concepts illustrate the frequency of...
- This is evidence of the key role...
- The major elements of these ideas indicate that...

Negative Phrasing

- The limitations of the ideas expressed indicate...
- The main shortcomings of this approach are...
- The probability of the impact is questionable...

Nuanced Phrasing

Arguments are essentially viewpoints that need to be substantiated. This is achieved with caution, focus, generality, objectivity and by using nuanced language. Here are some examples of nuanced words and phrases:

- The likelihood is...
- It appears that...
- There is a degree if certainty that...
- There seems to be a credible link between X and y, as indicated by Hewitt et al. (2017)

Encouraging Fluency in Your Writing

To ensure that your writing has flow, appears well organised and is logical and-structured, please consider the following steps:

1 Ensure that your paragraphs identify a key discussion area.
2 Introduce your paragraph with a topic sentence.
3 Form links within your paragraphs with key connecting words.
4 Ensure that your concluding sentence within the paragraph refreshes the reader of your key points.
5 Follow the next paragraph with a linking sentence. (Cottrell, 2005)

Building Connection in Your Work

Connecting your ideas and paragraphs so that there is a strong narrative flow is important for the fluency of your writing. Here are some words and phrases you can use to do so:

- **Comparing ideas:** Similarly, in comparison, likewise
- **Contrasting ideas:** In contrast, on the other hand, in spite of.
- **Explanations:** In other words, to be more precise.
- **Supportive statements:** Indeed, as a matter of fact, in reality.

- **Statement of fact:** Clearly, naturally, surely.
- **Concluding statements:** In summary, overall, to conclude.

Other phrases you may find helpful include:

- Initially it would appear...
- The most important theme...
- Furthermore...
- In addition to...
- Owing to the fact...
- Consequently...
- As a result of which...

Generating Comparison and Contrast in Your Writing

An important aspect of academic writing is to achieve depth to your discussion points. The ability to compare and contrast the themes you present are crucial. What this essentially means is to examine the similarities and differences of the ideas you present.

> **Top Tip:** Use of comparison words include:
> however, than, and, is unlike, greater than...

Applying Supportive Claims in Your Writing

Making a substantiated generalisation in your writing is key alongside supportive claims. Words and phrases such as 'this is shown by/demonstrated by/indicated by/illustrated by' indicate a supportive claim.

Drawing Conclusions....

After your ideas have been presented, an evaluation of the themes outlined and-supported by key evidence, the conclusion acts to definitively reinforce the aim of the piece of work has been successfully achieved.

As well as a summary your conclusions can act to suggest new ideas and make recommendations. It aims to bring your work to a whole, to form a clear picture. Suggested language for writing your conclusions include:

- The evidence strongly recommends that. . .
- The ideas suggest that it is advisable to. . .
- In conclusion. . .
- On the basis of the evidence presented. . .

Are You Writing Critically? Double Check....

In developing your arguments, you can use your lecture notes and key texts but please ensure:

- You use your notes from your lectures and reading but paraphrase your ideas (put your own ideas and words into your discussion points from the sources you have read).
- You extend your discussion points, link it to another idea and question it in depth. Ideas should never be left in isolation but link to your key themes and ideas, with extension and flow throughout your work.

Action: Developing your own voice in your writing is crucial – how will you look to develop this process further?
Initially it would appear. . .
The most important theme. . .
Furthermore. . .
In addition to. . . Owing to the fact, Consequently. . .
As a result of which. . .
Activity: Check your understanding of key terms used in academic writing.
To assess:
Give careful consideration to all the factors or events that apply and identify which are the most important and relevant, with reasons.
To critically analyse:
Give your view after you have considered all the evidence, particularly the importance of both the relevant and positive and negative aspects.

Comprehensively explain:
Give a very detailed explanation that covers all the relevant points and give reasons for your views or actions.
To critically evaluate:
Review the information to decide the degree to which something is true, important or valuable. Then assess the possible alternatives, taking into account their strengths and weaknesses if they were applied instead. Then give a precise and detailed account to explain your opinion. Use SOY: Some said, Others said, You think.
To summarise:
Identify/review the main relevant factors and/or arguments so that these are explained in a clear and concise manner.

Use of a Phrasebank

Our choice of phrasing in academic writing is crucial. In this chapter we have covered a wide range of words and phrases to support your writing. You can go further by using an online phrasebook which covers many more examples.

Top Tip: An excellent source that demonstrates useful examples of this is from the University of Manchester: http://www.phrasebank.manchester.ac.uk/being-critical/

6

Editing, Proof Reading and Referencing Your Work

Key Points

Together in Chapter 6, we will examine and explore the following themes:

- The value editing holds.
- Consider your use of grammar, punctuation and spelling.
- The importance of referencing.
- Why we reference.
- Useful resources.

It takes considerable time and effort to research and compile your work. One of the key and final steps is to ensure you have adhered to the guidelines and your work is edited, proofread, presented and referenced effectively.

Top Tip: First impressions make a lasting impression!

Depending on the requirements of the assignment brief, you will need to have a title page and that your work is presented in the right order. You will need to consider the type and size of font required, the line spacing and consider how your writing looks on the printed page – your line spacing, text justification, the font, layout, paragraph structure and use of margins are crucial. Ensure you have page numbers; these are crucial for your

Lecturer to follow the correct sequence. Ensure that you have checked for any spelling and grammatical errors and that your references are included and the correct referencing system is used. Similarly, you will need to assess if you need to provide a plagiarism and confidentiality statement. Let's look at these key themes in more detail.

The Value Editing Holds

Editing and proof reading your work is crucial. It is best done, step by step, piece by piece. Plan to leave yourself several days to give yourself enough time to review your work.

Whilst editing your work can be time consuming, it is well worth the effort. It can really enhance the quality of your work and is useful to enable you to reflect on your efforts and to develop yourself as a writer.

When we compile a well written piece, that is valued, the benefits to us personally and professionally are without question. Ultimately it enables us to communicate our ideas with greater clarity.

When editing your work, you are essentially looking to compare your work to the assignment with a critical eye.

Activity: Ask yourself if you think you have answered the question set:

- How well do you communicate your ideas?
- Do you give clarity, structure and cohesion to your arguments?
- How have you examined ways of finding and indicating your own ideas through those of others.
- Does your work hold structure, flow and relevance to the assignment?
- Found ways of giving clarity to your work through your choice of key words in your writing.
- Have you presented your ideas objectively? Re-read your work for any missing's and spot key mistakes?

Consider Your Use of Grammar, Punctuation and Spelling

It is crucial that your work is presented accurately, that you use full sentences and punctuation throughout your work and that allow your sentences to be broken into key parts to assist with flow of argument. Use your spell checker to correct spellings, but notice unusual errors that spell check may fall short on.

Punctuation

- Full stops (.) show the end of a sentence
- Commas (,) add pauses to sentences allowing the reader to draw breath. Are you using these correctly?
- Apostrophes (') show possession
- Quotation marks (") illustrate the work of others
- Colons (:) add information after a statement or clause.
- Semi-colons (;) separate items in lists

In addition to spelling and punctuation, there are some other key things to spot check during your edit, listed below.

- Does your work demonstrate both sides of an argument before reaching an ultimate conclusion based on evidence?
- Do your discussion points express your interpretation of ideas and synthesise them (i.e. apply these to your own context).
- Is your work within the word count? Many universities no longer apply the plus or minus ten per cent rule.
- Ensure that your work does not include text speak.
- Ensure that you do not use questions or exclamation marks in your discussion points.

Action: Work through the check points above step by step.
Does your work explore the lines of argument fairly and equally?
Do you need to correct any imbalances?
Top Tip: Ensure that your ideas are always supported by evidence.

The Importance of Referencing

Referencing is important to demonstrate that you are writing effectively and honestly. The idea being to reference the concepts and words of other writers that you have used in producing your work. It is important to remember that when we cite evidence that we have utilised from reading or research we *must* reference it.

Osmond (2013) defines referencing as: 'a system used to make clear to the reader when you are bringing ideas, words, quotes, illustrations, concepts or anything from other sources into your own assignments'.

Why We Reference Literature

References are required to substantiate and acknowledge the source of the literature within your work to highlight a discussion point or argument. Your academic argument will be stronger if it's supported by evidence from others' research and others will be able to find and use the same sources that informed your work, which in turn allows them to check the validity and authenticity of your work, as well as develop and enhance their own understanding of the subject. Similarly, identifying your sources helps you avoid plagiarism by attributing the contribution of others to your work. Note that there is a subtle difference between a reference list, which details in alphabetical order by author surname all of the material you have referred to in your work, and a bibliography, which details literature of relevance to your work but includes that which you may not have explicitly used in the body of your writing.

In addition to showing that you have read around a subject, references are helpful to your academic writing by providing opportunities to present a particular perspective or counterargument, as well as to validate your own arguments.

Referencing Systems

As you will probably have identified, there are many referencing systems or styles, each with similarities and differences. The aim of all of the systems is the same – to act as an indicator of other ideas. All sources must be referenced, according to the educational institutions preferred style. Please utilise the preferred academic referencing system indicated to you by your own higher education organisation. As an example, one of the most common systems used is the Harvard method.

Individual University and School Policies

Universities each have their own referencing policies and requirements of their students, and different schools or departments within the university may require the use of specific referencing styles. It is important to check and confirm which referencing style (e.g., APA, MLA, Harvard, Chicago) is required by your school or department before you begin your writing. Following the correct style ensures consistency and adherence to academic standards and the requirements of your programme of study.

When to Reference

You should reference whenever you use an idea from someone else's work, whether it comes from a journal article, textbook, website, or any other source. This is essential even if you:

- **Paraphrase** the idea by putting it into your own words.
- **Summarise** the key points of their work.
- **Directly quote** their exact words.

Referencing in all these cases is crucial for maintaining academic integrity and ensuring clarity about which ideas are your own and which are derived from others. This is a fundamental aspect of good practice in academic writing.

How to Reference

There are a number of useful resources to help you reference using a variety of different styles. Below are some examples:

MyBib (https://www.mybib.com). This is a useful free tool that creates accurate citations for books, journal, websites and videos in over 9,000 styles. You can search by title or identifier and download to Microsoft Word.

Cite Them Right (https://www.citethemrightonline.com). This is another helpful resource helping you to reference appropriately according to the style that your university requires.

> **Action Point:** Select a piece of work that you have used in your writing; it could be a website, journal or book. Visit MyBib (https://www.mybib.com) and use it to create a reference.

Plagiarism

Plagiarism is using the work of other people to gain some form of benefit, without formally acknowledging that the work came from someone else.

We often develop ideas from things we hear about, see and read.

Plagiarism is a deliberate attempt to pass off someone else's ideas as your own.

Changing work into your own words does not make it your work.

Submission of an essay via university systems provides a similarity check. When you submit your work, you will see the similarity report.

Referencing Tools

Do you find referencing tricky and doubt yourself even when you have compiled your reference list?

In this case, you may wish to use the reference guide within Microsoft word, click on *references* in the tool bar.

Harvard Cite Them Right is also another useful tool. Choose your preferred style of referencing from the dropdown menu and insert citation.

Both are easy to use and accurate.

Let's Summarise

Doing your final edit is a good chance to review all aspects of your work, so let's remind ourselves of what to check.

Critical Writing

In developing your arguments, you can use your lecturer's notes and key texts but please ensure:

You use your notes from your lectures and reading but paraphrase your ideas (put your own ideas and words into your discussion points from the sources you have read.

You extend your discussion points, link it to another idea and question it in depth. Ideas should never be left in isolation but link it to your key themes and ideas, with extension and flow throughout your work.

Developing your own voice in your writing is crucial.

Fluency of Writing

To ensure that your writing has flow, appears well organised and is logical and structured, please consider the following steps:

Ensure that your paragraphs identify a key discussion area.

Introduce your paragraph with a topic sentence.

Form links within your paragraphs with key connecting words.

Ensure that your concluding sentence within the paragraph refreshes the reader of your key points.

Follow the next paragraph with a linking sentence.

Demonstrating Evaluations

Alongside a demonstration of your own viewpoint, it is important to evaluate ideas. The best way to achieve this is to produce evidence and explain why this evidence lies in support of your own point of view.

As a Further Reminder

- Deliver your point of view
- Emphasise the positive aspects of your ideas
- Examine the negative aspects
- Evaluate the themes you present

Arguing Viewpoints

Arguments are essentially viewpoints that need to be substantiated. Often in academic writing this is achieved with caution, focus, generality and objectivity. The language style is crucial. The following is an illustrated example of this:

There seems to be a credible link between…as indicated by Hewitt et al., 2017.

Please note that the language style and the formality it offers, without using the first person. Other example phrases to extend your critical writing style are:

rather, probable, the likelihood is, it appears that, it would appear to have a degree of certainty that…

Conclusions

After your ideas have been presented, an evaluation of the themes outlined and supported by key evidence, the conclusion acts to definitively reinforce the aim of the piece of work has been successfully achieved.

As well as a summary of your conclusions can act to suggest new ideas and make recommendations. It aims to bring your work to a whole, to form a clear picture.

Top Tips: Key language in concluding your ideas are as follows:
The evidence strongly recommends that...
The ideas suggest that it is advisable to...
In conclusion...
On the basis of the evidence presented...

Summary

Together we have looked at a range of themes that guide you in your academic writing journey.

Chapter 1: Learning to Learn
- We explore the purpose of academic writing.
- Knowledge areas required within the healthcare professions.
- The skills to build, demonstrate and apply our knowledge.
- Demystifying the requirements of the terminology in your assignment criteria.
- Ways of developing effective reading and note taking methods.

Chapter 2: Getting Into the Mindset for Independent Study
- Think about things differently by redefining your mindset and method.
- Becoming an active and effective learner who takes a deeper dive.
- Know thyself and your learning style.
- Developing a critical mindset.
- Using critically reflective tools to enhance your practice.

Chapter 3: Planning for Academic Writing
- How to source and effectively evaluate literature.
- Develop your critical thinking skills.
- Effectively evaluate your chosen sources.

Chapter 4: Examining Different Writing Styles for Different Purposes
- Examine differences in various writing styles.

- Understand the distinction of working between writing in the personal/ subjective reflection and critical reflection.
- Identify the requirements of an essay, report, personal and reflective writing.
- Identify key sources to support your writing skills.

Chapter 5: Developing Your Critical Writing Skills and Structuring Critical Argument

- What academic writing requires.
- The importance of critical thinking and creating arguments – weighing it all up.
- How to give clarity to the ideas you present via your choice of key words.
- Examining check points for creating and deconstructing argument and enhancing your critical thinking skills.
- The application of critical writing and how to effectively structure your work and robustly articulate your arguments, with check points and examples.
- Carefully selecting keywords to demonstrate your ideas and to enhance the flow of your points.

Chapter 6: Editing, Proof Reading and Referencing Your Work

- The value editing holds.
- Considering your use of grammar, punctuation and spelling.
- The importance of referencing.
- Why we reference.
- Useful resources.

Remember, your preparation, approach and careful thought and mindful application of ideas are key to your success. You are advised to plan your time well, building on your ideas step by step, using quality sources, formulating your arguments within a defined framework, seeking feedback from others and continuously proof reading your work as you go. Remember that writing the perfect piece is like drawing the perfect circle. Meaning that no matter what you do you'll always end up with a zero? Not meaning it's impossible, but with the right tools, you can get pretty darn close.

Wishing you every success, Deborah Miarkowska.

Bibliography

Argyris, C. (1993). *Knowledge for action. A guide to overcoming barriers to organizational change*. Jossey-Bass Publishers.

Anderson, L. W., Krathwohl, D. R., Airasian, P., Cruikshank, K., Mayer, R., Pintrich, P., Raths, J., & Wittrock, M. (Eds.). (2001). *A taxonomy for learning, teaching, and assessing: A revision of bloom's taxonomy of educational objectives*. Allyn & Bacon. Pearson Education Group.

Barnett, R. (2011). *Being a university*. Routledge.

Barrett, G. (2004). Bullying and harassment at work: Time to take action. *Journal of Neonatal Nursing, 10*(2).

Bart, C. K., & Baetz, M. C. (1998). The relationship between mission statements and firm performance: An exploratory study. *Journal of Management Studies, 35*, 823–853.

Bart, C. K., Bontis, N., & Taggar, S. (2001). A model of the impact of mission statements on firm performance. *Management Decision, 39*(1), 19–35.

Bloom, B. S. (1956). *Taxonomy of educational objectives, handbook: The cognitive domain*. David McKay.

Bolden, R., Gosling, J., O'Brien, A., Peters, K., Ryan, M. K., Haslam, S. A., & Winklemann, K. (2012). *Academic leadership: Changing conceptions, identities and experiences in UK higher education*. Leadership Foundation for Higher Education.

Borton, T. (1970). *Reach, touch and teach*. McGraw-Hill.

Burkus, D., (2014). *How to tell if your company has a creative culture*. https://hbr.org/2014/12/how-to-tell-if-your-company-has-a-creative-culture. Accessed on May 01, 2018.

Caldwell, R. (2005). Leadership & Learning. A critical re-examination of Senge's learning organization. Systematic practice and action. *SPARFL, 18*(4), 335–434. ISSN.1094-429X.

Carper, B. A. (1978). Fundamental patterns of knowing in nursing. *Advances in Nursing Science, 1*(1), 13–24.

CASP. *Critical appraisal skills programme*. https://casp-uk.net/casp-tools-checklists/

Chinn, L.P., & Kramer, K.M. (2015). *Knowledge development in nursing, theory & process*. Elsevier Press.

Chinn, P. L., Kramer, M., & Sitzman, K. (2022). *Knowledge development in nursing: Theory and process* (11th ed.). Elsevier.

CIPD. (2013). *Real life leaders: Closing the knowing-doing gap*. Chartered institute of personal development.

Cottrell, S. (2005). *Critical thinking skills: Developing effective analysis and argument.* Palgrave Study Skills.

Covey, S. R. (2004). *The 7 habits of highly effective people: Restoring the character ethic.* Free Press.

Croskerry, P., Cosby, K.S., Schenkel, S. & Wears, R. (2008). *Patient safety in emergency medicine.* Lippincott, Williams & Wilkins.

Cross, R., Ernst, C., & Passmore, B. (2013). A bridge too far? How boundary spanning networks drive organizational change and effectiveness. *Organizational Dynamics, 42*(2), 81–91.

Curtis, E., & O'Connell, R. (2011). Essential leadership skills for motivating and developing staff. *Nursing Management, 18*(5), 32–35.

Denby, N., Butroyd, R., Swift, H., Price, J., Glazzard, J. & Avis, J. (2008). *Masters level study in education: A guide to success for PGCE students.* Open University Press.

Dewey, J. (1910). How we think. *The Journal of Education, 71*(17). (1777) April 28, 1970, p. 468.

Dooley, L. (2017). *Corporate Leadership for economic and social change.* https://books. google.co.uk/books?hl=en&lr=&id=Oqo0DwAAQBAJ&oi=fnd&pg=PA30&dq=doo ley+2017+leadership&ots=4DYi2p85Nd&sig=oX3HS6zVNfzRsBo-wo1p83n2ebs#v =onepage&q=dooley%202017%20leadership&f=false. Accessed on Monday 20 May, 2024.

Druker, P. F. (2005). *Critical evaluations in business & management.* Edited by Wood, J. C. and Wood, M. C. Routledge.

Dweck, C. S. (2010). Mind-sets and equitable education. *Principal Leadership, 10,* 26–29.

Dweck, C. S. (2012). *Mindset: How you can fulfil your potential.* Constable & Robinson.

Dweck, C. S. (2015). Growth. *British Journal of Psychology, 85,* 242–245.

Eagly, A. H. (2005). *Achieving relational authenticity; Does Gender matter?* https://www. scholars.northwestern.edu/en/publications/achieving-relational-authenticity-in-leader ship-does-gender-matter. Accessed on April 30, 2018.

Erikson, T. J. (2010, May). The Leaders we need now. *Harvard Business Review,* 63–66. https://hbr.org/2010/05/the-leaders-we-need-now. Accessed on May 04, 2018.

Ernst, C., & Chrobot-Mason, D. (2011). Flat world, hard boundaries – How to lead across them. *MIT Sloan Management Review, 52*(3), 81–88.

Ernst, C., & Chrobot-Mason, D. (2011b). *Boundary spanning leadership. Six Practices for solving problems. Driving innovation and transforming organizations. Centre for creative leadership.* McGraw Hill.

Fleck, R. (2012). Rating reflection on experience: A case study of teachers' and tutors' reflection around images. *Interacting with Computers. 24*(6), 439–449. https://doi.org/10.1016/j.intcom.2012.07.003

Forsyth, D. R. (2010). *Group dynamics* (5th ed.). Wadsworth Cengage Learning. ISBN 9780495599524.

Francis, D. L. (2020). *Exploiting agility for advantage.* De Gruyter Press.

The Francis Report. (2013). http://webarchive.nationalarchives.gov.uk/20150407084003/http://www.midstaffspublicinquiry.com/. Accessed on May 05, 2018.

George, B. (2007). Why leaders lose their way, *Strategy & Leadership, 35*(3), 4–11. https://doi.org/10.1108/10878570710745776. Accessed on April 21, 2018.

Gibb, A., Haskins, G., Hannon, P., &Robertson, I. (2012). *Leading the entrepreneurial university.* National Centre for Entrepreneurship in Education. http://eureka.sbs.ox.ac.uk/4861/. Accessed on January 10, 2019.

Gill, R. (2011). *Theory and practice of leadership* (2nd ed.). Sage.

Gillett, A., Hammond, A. & Martala, M. (2009). *Inside Track. Successful academic writing.* Pearson Education.

Goleman, D. (2000). Emotional intelligence leadership. *Harvard Business Review.* https://hbr.org/2000/03/leadership-that-gets-results

Goleman, D., Cherniss, C., Extein, M. & Weissberg, R.P. (2006). 'Emotional intelligence: what does the research really indicate?', *Educational Psychologist, 41*(4), 239–245.

Gopee, N. (2015). *Mentoring and supervision in healthcare.* SAGE.

Gopee, N. (2022). *Leading and Managing Healthcare.* Sage.

Gough, V. (2018). *Which model should I use.* https://www.trainingzone.co.uk/lead/culture/organisational-change-which-model-should-i-use. Accessed on November 18, 2020.

Gregory, A., & Willis, P. (2013). *Strategic public relations leadership.* Routledge.

Grunig, J. E. (1992). Communication, public relations and effective organisations: An overview of the book. In J. E. Grunig (Ed.), *Excellence in public relations and communication management.* Lawrence Erlbaum Associates.

Hayes, J. (2007). *The theory and practice of change management.* Palgrave Macmillan.

Heath, R. L. (2001). Shifting foundations: Public relations as relationship building. In R. L. Heath (Ed.), *The Sage handbook of public relations.* SAGE.

Hiatt, J. M., & Creasey, T. J. Change management, the people side of change. Prosci Learning Center Publications.

Huczynski, A., & Buchanan David, A. (2019). *Organizational behaviour.* Pearson.

Johnson, G., & Scholes, K. (1999). *Exploring corporate strategy* (5th ed.). Prentice Hall.

Jones, B. F., & Olken, B. A. (2005). *Do leaders matter? National leadership & growth since World War II.* https://economics.mit.edu/files/2915. Accessed on May 04 2018.

Katrak, P., Bialocerkowski, A., Massy-Westropp, N.M. & Kumar, S. (2004). A systematic review of the content of critical appraisal tools. Researchgate. *BMC Medical Research Methodology*, *4*(1), 22. https://doi.org/10.1186/1471-2288-4-22

Kavanaugh, E. 2017. *Exploring the Kotter model and appreciative inquiry as organisational change vehicles for non-profit human services agencies*. http://www.earonkavanagh.ca/kavanagh_article-exploring.pdf. Accessed in October 2019.

Kearns, D. (2005). *Team of rivals: The political genius of Abraham Lincoln*. Simon & Schuster.

Kolb, D. (1984). *Experiential learning: Experience as the source of learning and development*. Prentice-Hall. ISBN: 0132952610.

Kotter, J. P. (1996). *Leading change*. Harvard Business School Press.

Kowalski, T. J. (2008). *Public relations in schools* (4th ed.). Pearson Education.

Lee, L., Magellen Horth, D., & Ernst, C. (2014). *Boundary Spanning in action – Tactics for transforming today's borders into tomorrow's frontiers*. Center for Creative Leadership.

Lovatt, A. (2014, May) Defining critical thoughts. *Nurse Education Today*. *34*(5), 670–672. https://doi.org/10.1016/j.nedt.2013.12.003. Accessed on December 27, 2013.

Lumby, J. (2012). Leading organizational culture: Issues of power & equity. *Journal of Educational Management Administration & Leadership*, *40*(5), 576–591.

McClelland, D. C. (1987). *Human motivation*. Cambridge University Press.

McGuire, J. B., Palus, C. J., Pasmore, W., & Rhodes, G. B. (2009). *Transforming your organization*. Center for Creative Leadership.

Molero, F., Cuadrado, I., Navas, M., & Morales, J. F. (2007). Relations and effect of transformational leadership: A comparative analysis with traditional leadership styles. *The Spanish Journal of Psychology; Madrid*, *10*(2), 358–368.

Morely, J. (2023). *Academic Phrasebank. An academic writing resource for students and researchers*. University of Manchester.

Morrall, P., & Goodman, B. (2013). Critical thinking, nurse education and universities: Some thoughts on current issues and implications for nursing practice. *Nurse Education Today*. https://doi.org/10.1016/j.nedt.2012.11.011

Nayab (2010). *How does leadership affect group communication*. http://brighthubpm.com/resource-management/92791-how-does-leadership-affect--group-communication/. Accessed May 1, 2018.

NMC. (2018). *The Code. Professional Standards of practice and behaviour for nurses, midwives and nursing associates*. https://www.nmc.org.uk/standards/code/

Northhouse, P. G. (2016). *Leadership. Theory & practice* (7th ed.). SAGE.

Odell, J. (2015). Clinical decision making in minor illness. *Practice Nursing*, *26*(10).

Osmond, A. (2013). *Academic Writing and Grammar for students*. Sage.

Parrish, D. R. (2015). The relevance of emotional intelligence for leadership in a higher education context. *Studies in Higher Education, 40*(5), 821–837. https://doi.org/10. 1080/03075079.2013.842225

Price, B., & Harrington, A. (2019). *Critical thinking and writing for nursing students.* Learning Matters.

Prosci (2019). *Change management methodology.* https://www.prosci.com/resources/ articles/change-management-methodology. (Accessed on January 22, 2019).

Prysor, D., & Henley, A. (2017). *Boundary spanning in higher education leadership: Identifying boundaries and practices in a British University.* Studies in Higher Education. Routledge. https://www.tandfonline.com/doi/full/10.1080/03075079.2017. 1318364. Accessed on November, 1118.

Quang, N., N. (2022). Postlesson affordance-based reflective discussion in ELT classes. *TESOL Journal.* https://doi.org/10.1002/tesj.677

Ramsden, P. (1998). Managing the effective university. *Higher Education Research and Development, 17*(3), 347–370.

Rowntree. (1976). *Assessing students how shall we know them?* (pp. 40–64). Routledge.

Scholes, E., & James, D. (1997). Planning stakeholder communication. *Journal of Communication Management, 2*(3), 277–285.

Schon, D. (1993). *The reflective practitioner.* Iriss Press.

Seale, O., & Cross, M. (2015). Leading and managing in complexity: The case of South African Deans. *Studies in Higher Education.* https://doi.org/10.1080/03075079.2014. 988705

Senge, P. (1990). *The Art & Practice of the fifth discipline.* http://www.seeing-everything-in-a-new-way.com/uploads/2/8/5/1/28516163/peter-senge-the-fifth-discipline.pdf. Accessed on November 11, 2018.

Senge, P. M. (2014). *The fifth discipline fieldbook: Strategies and tools for building a learning organization.* Crown Business.

Shein, E., H. (2016). *Organisational culture & leadership.* Wiley.

Smythe, J. (2007). *The Chief Engagement officer: Turning hierarchy upside down to drive performance.* Gower.

Stark, J. S., Briggs, C. L., & Rowland-Poplawski, J. (2002). Curriculum leadership roles of chairpersons in continuously planning departments. *Research in Higher Education, 43*(3), 329–356.

Steyn, B. (2003). From strategy to corporate communication strategy: A conceptualization. *Journal of Communication Management, 8*(2), 168–183.

Steyn, B. (2005). From strategy to corporate communication strategy: A conceptualization. *Journal of Communication Management, 8*(2), 168–183.

Terry. (1993). *Leadership. Theory & practice* (7th ed.). SAGE. Cited in Northouse, P.G. 2016.

The King's Fund (2016). *Bringing together physical and mental health. A new frontier for integrated care*. https://www.kingsfund.org.uk/sites/default/files/field/field_publication_file/Bringing-together-Kings-Fund-March-2016_1.pdf. Accessed on October 31, 2018.

Universities UK. (2015). *Patterns and trends in UK universities*. https://www.universitie suk.ac.uk/facts-and-stats/data-and-analysis/Pages/patterns-and-trends-uk-higher-education-2015.aspx. Accessed on January 11, 2019.

Vroom, V. H. (2003). Educating managers in decision making and leadership. *Management Decision, 10*, 968–978.

Weerts, D. J., & Sandmann, L. R. (2010). Community engagement and boundary spanning roles at research universities. *The Journal of Higher Education, 81*(6), 702–727.

West, M.A., & Chowla, R. (2017). Compassionate leadership for compassionate health care. In P. Gilbert (Ed.), *Compassion: Concepts, Research and Applications*. Routledge. pp. 237–257.

West, M. (2021). *Compassionate leadership: Susatianing wisdom, humanity and presence in health and social care*.

Willis, S. (2010). *Reflective practice for paramedics*. Research Gate. https://www.resea rchgate.net/publication/294292862_Reflective_Practice_for_Paramedics

Yip, J., & Ernst, C. & Campbell, M. (2015). *Boundary spanning leadership. Mission critical perspectives from the executive suite*. White Paper. https://www.ccl.org. Accessed on December 27, 2018.

Yip, J., Ernst, C., & Campbell (2016). *Boundary spanning leadership: Mission critical perspectives from the executive suite*. Centre for Creative Leadership.

Index